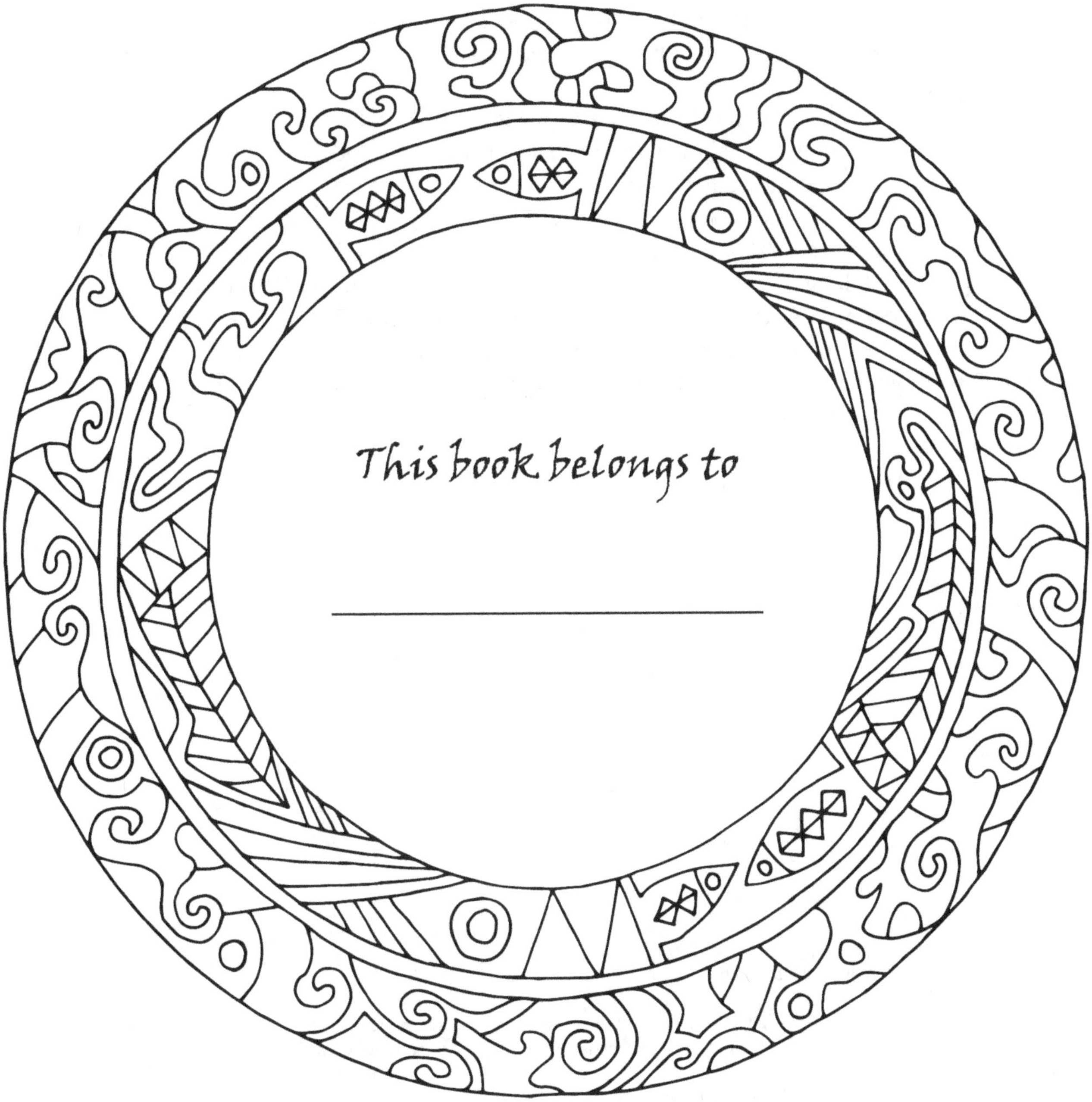

This book belongs to

_____

© 2021 Demitrius Lam. All rights reserved.

Artist Personal Message

Firstly, a sincere thank you for supporting an independent artist's work. I hope this will be as enjoyable to you as it has been to me conceptualizing and illustrating this book.

Illustrating and coloring these pages have also brought me much relaxation and calmness and clarity of the mind and I am sure they will bring to you the same.

Each artwork is specifically made on single sided page and with matching grey line version for your freedom to apply different techniques. If you are using wet media or highly saturated colors, I recommend putting a bloting sheet of paper in between the page you are coloring and the following page to ensure there is no bleed through to the next page.

Have a good time.

Copyright © 2021 Demitrius Lam

All rights reserved. No portion of this book may be reproduced in any form without permission from the publisher, except as permitted by U.S. copyright law.

For permissions contact: theavenuebay@gmail.com

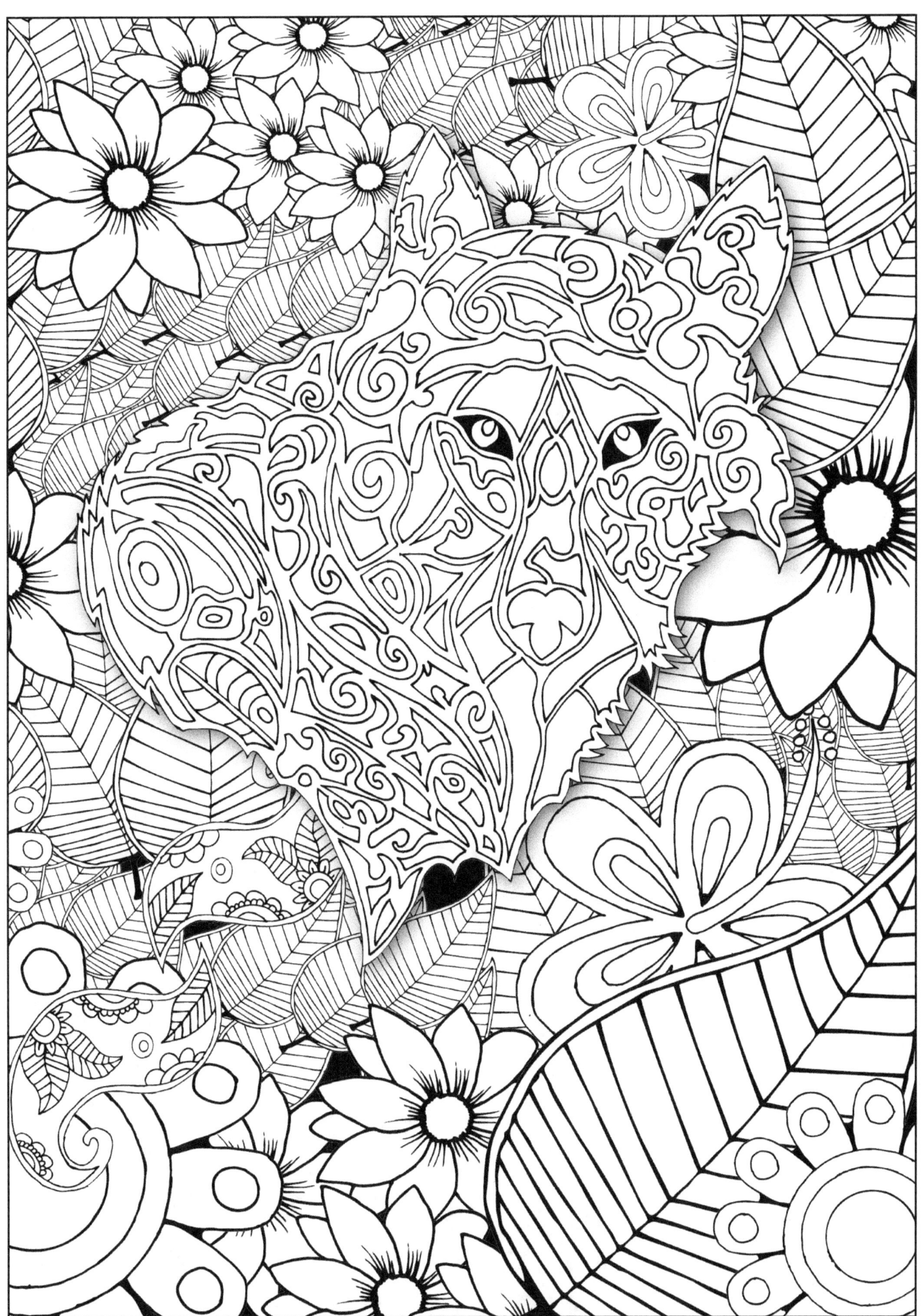

© 2021 Demitrius Lam. All rights reserved.

© 2021 Demitrius Lam. All rights reserved.

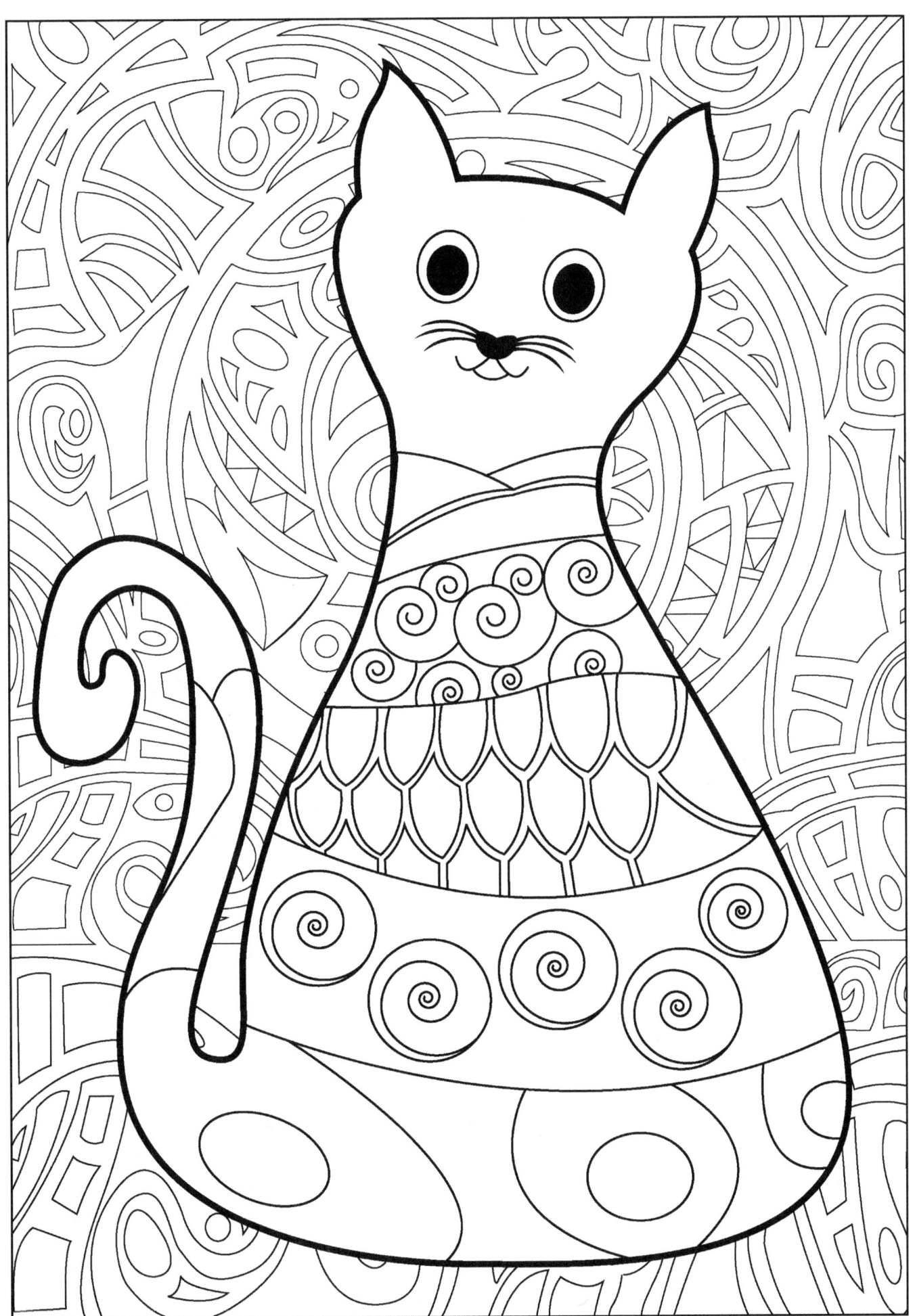

© 2021 Demitrius Lam. All rights reserved.

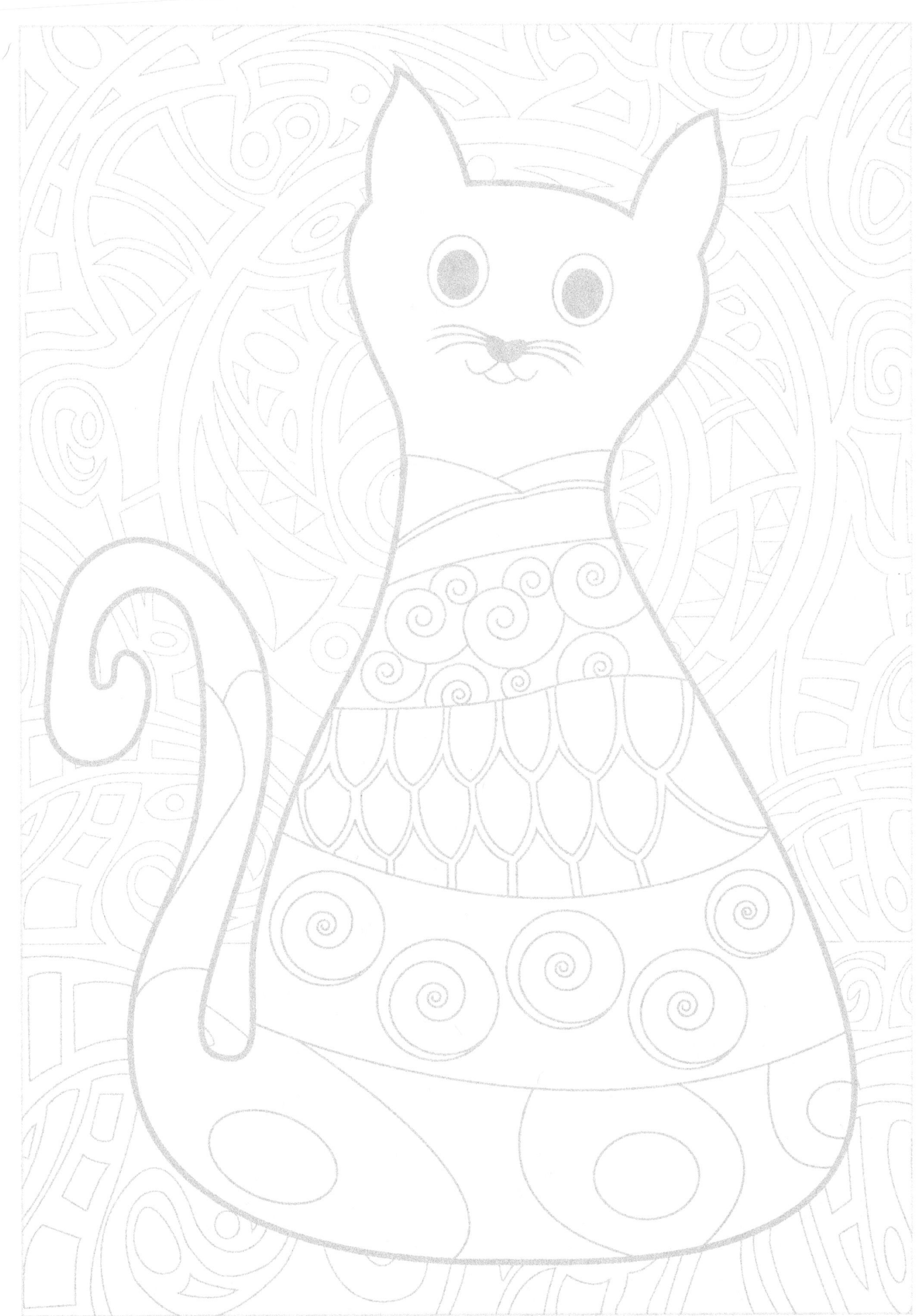

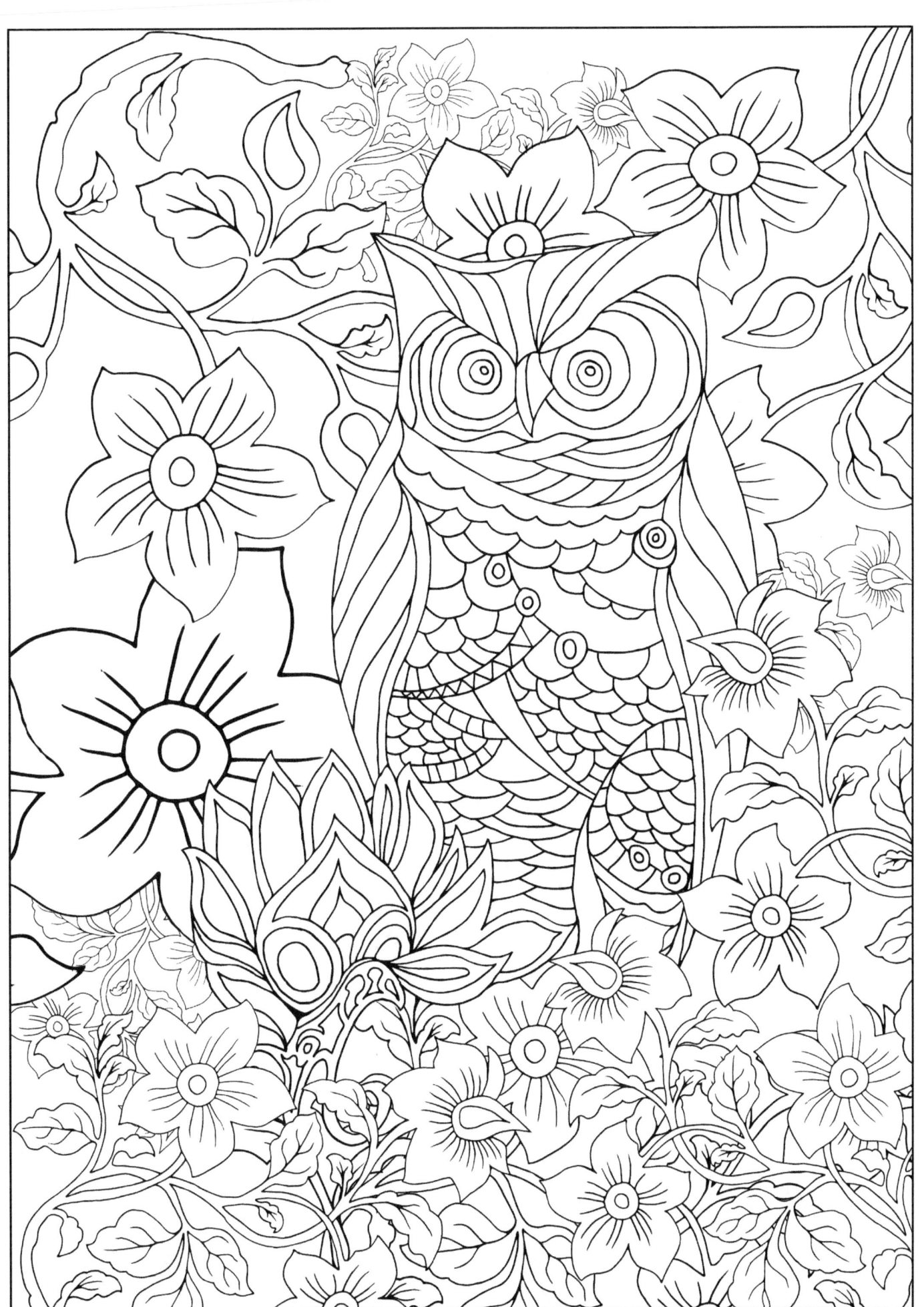

© 2021 Demitrius Lam. All rights reserved.

© 2021 Demitrius Lam. All rights reserved.

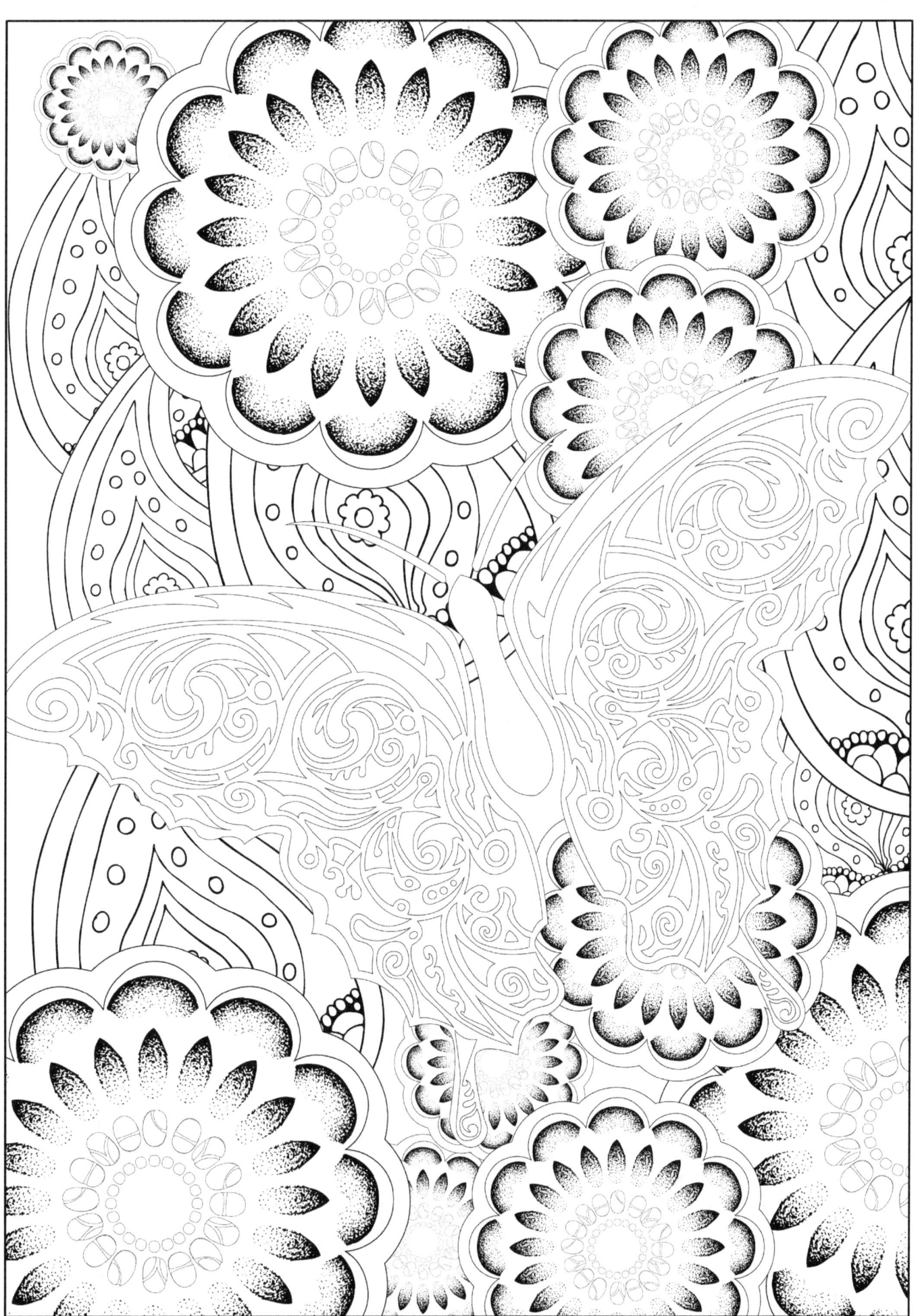
© 2021 Demitrius Lam. All rights reserved.

© 2021 Demitrius Lam. All rights reserved.

© 2021 Demitrius Lam. All rights reserved.

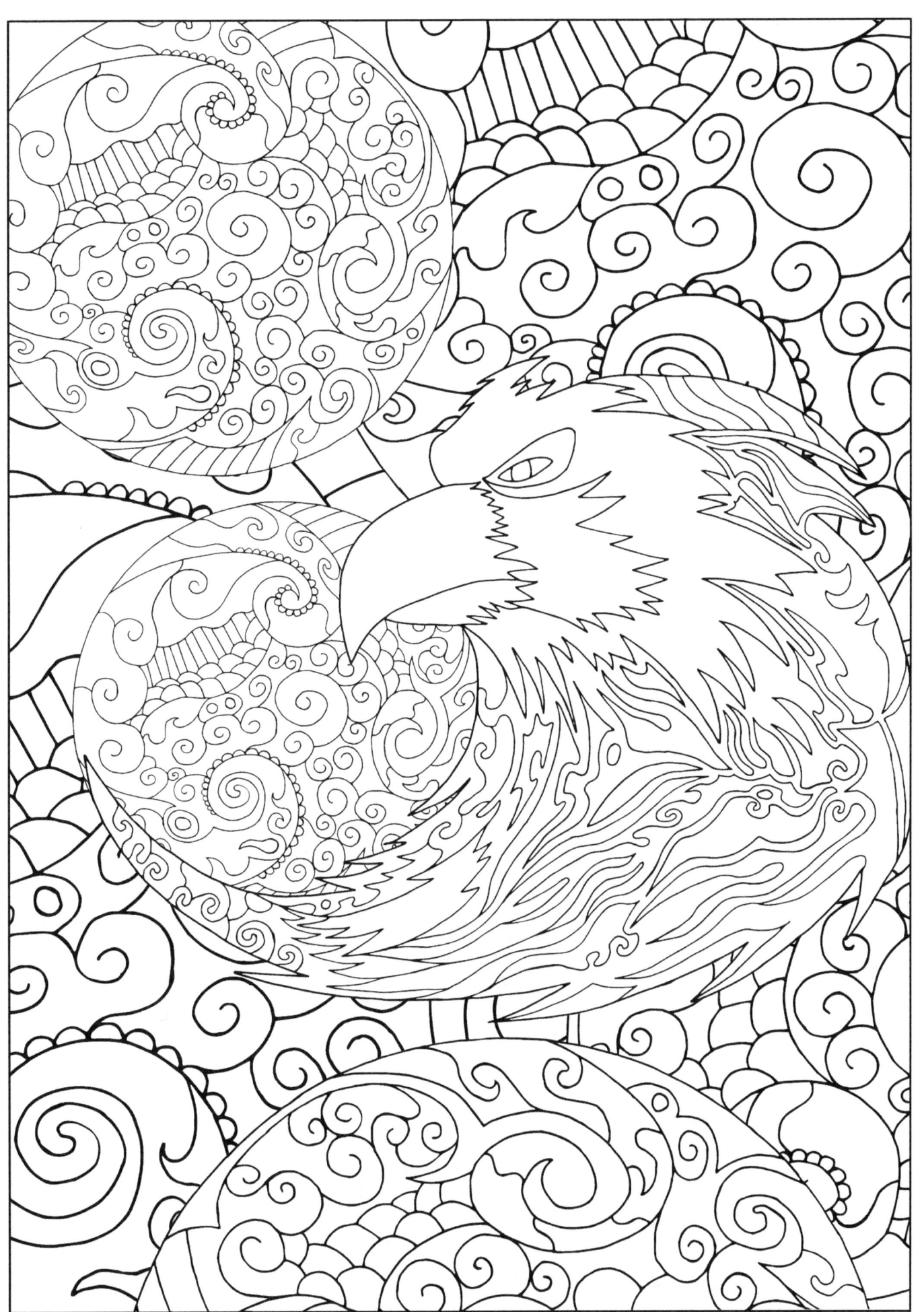

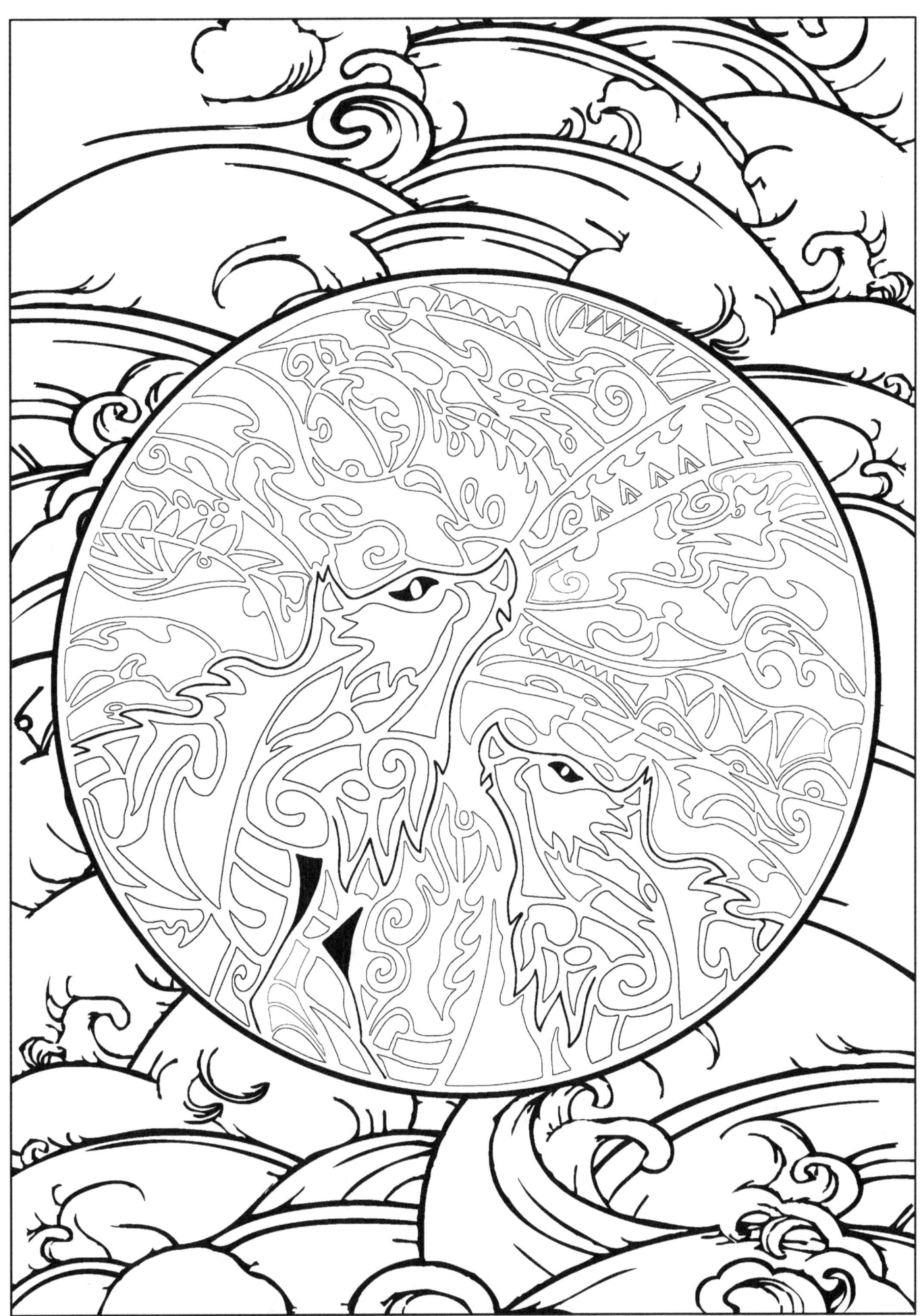

© 2021 Demitrius Lam. All rights reserved.

© 2021 Demitrius Lam. All rights reserved.

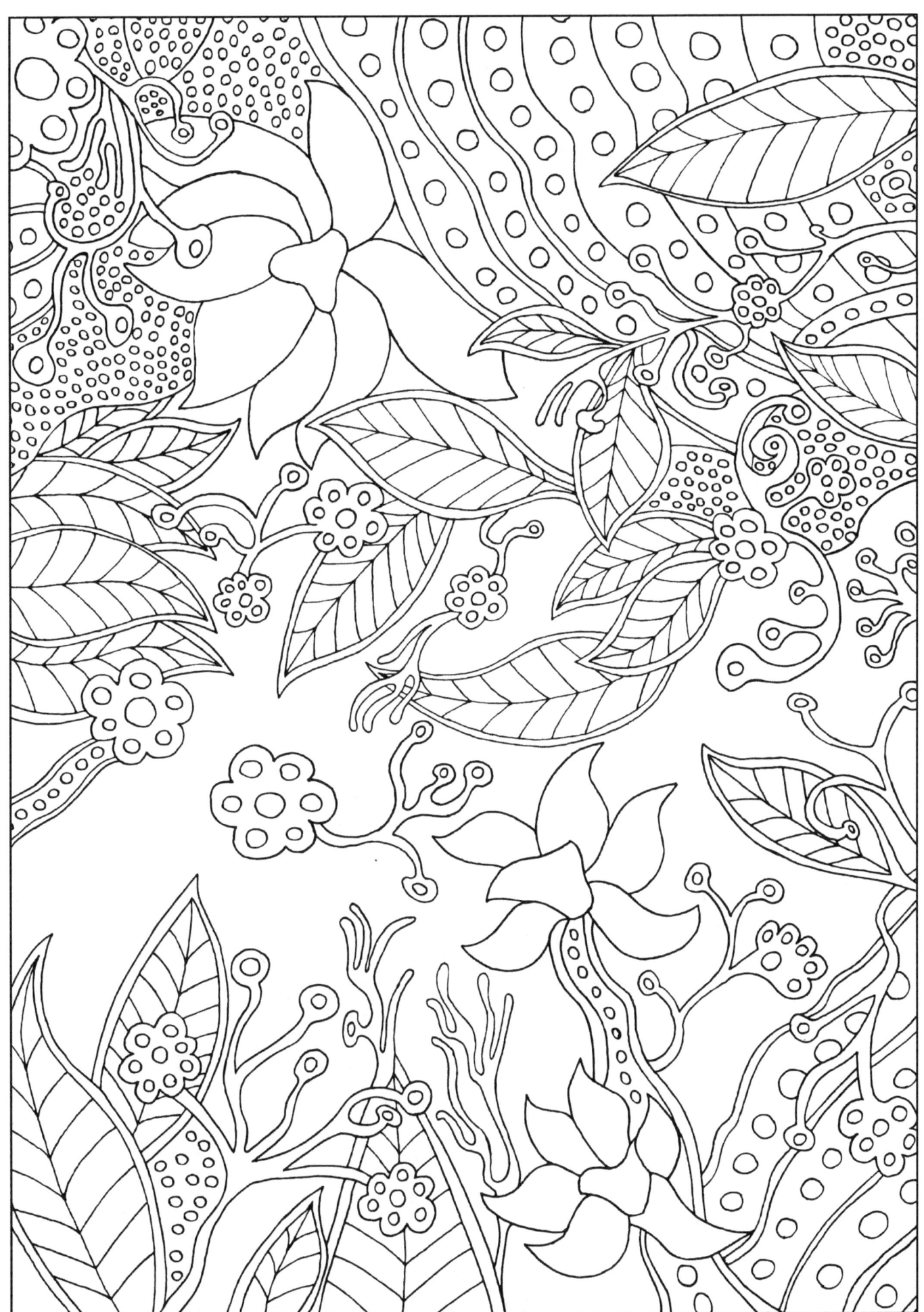

© 2021 Demitrius Lam. All rights reserved.

© 2021 Demitrius Lam. All rights reserved.

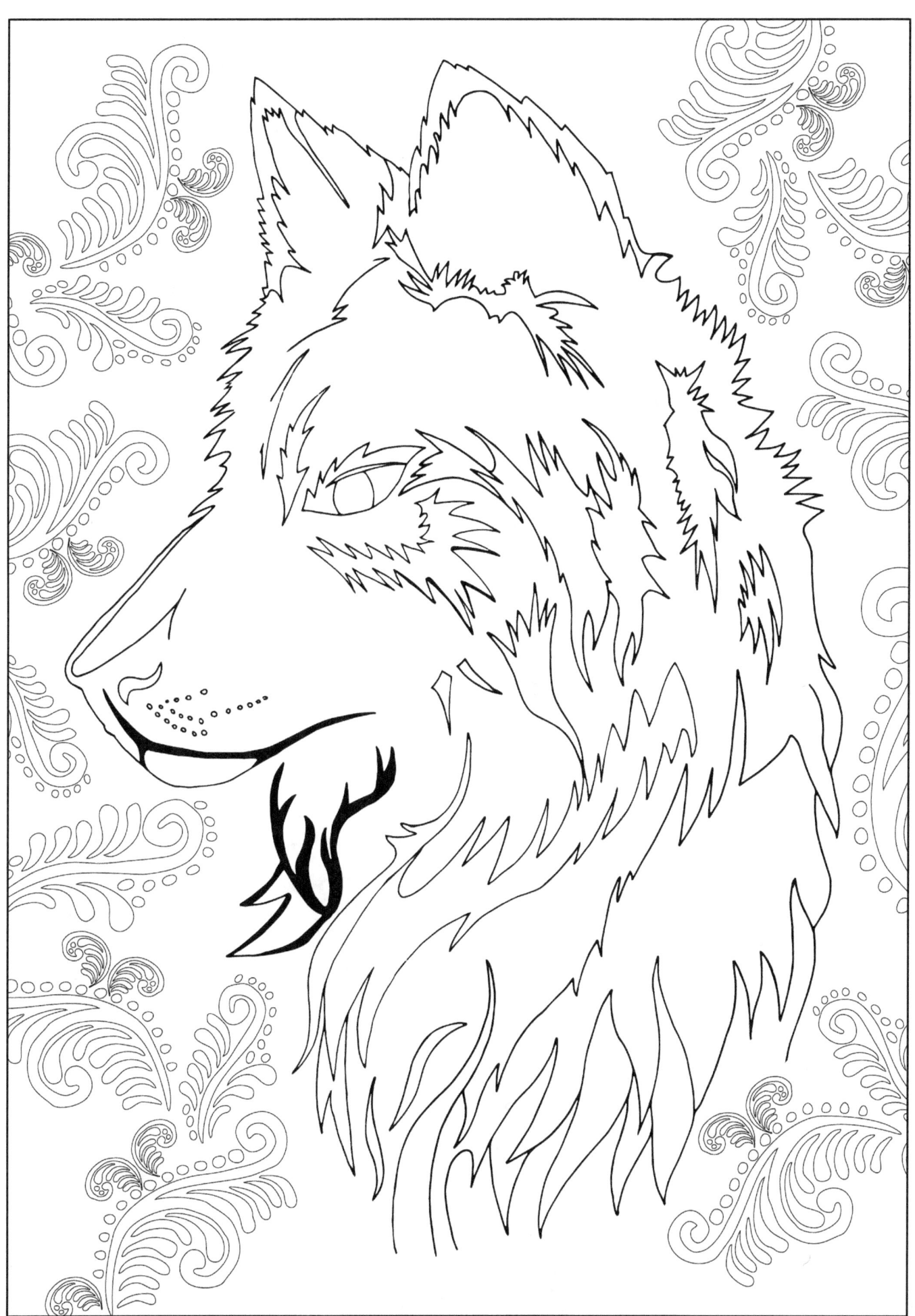

© 2021 Demitrius Lam. All rights reserved.

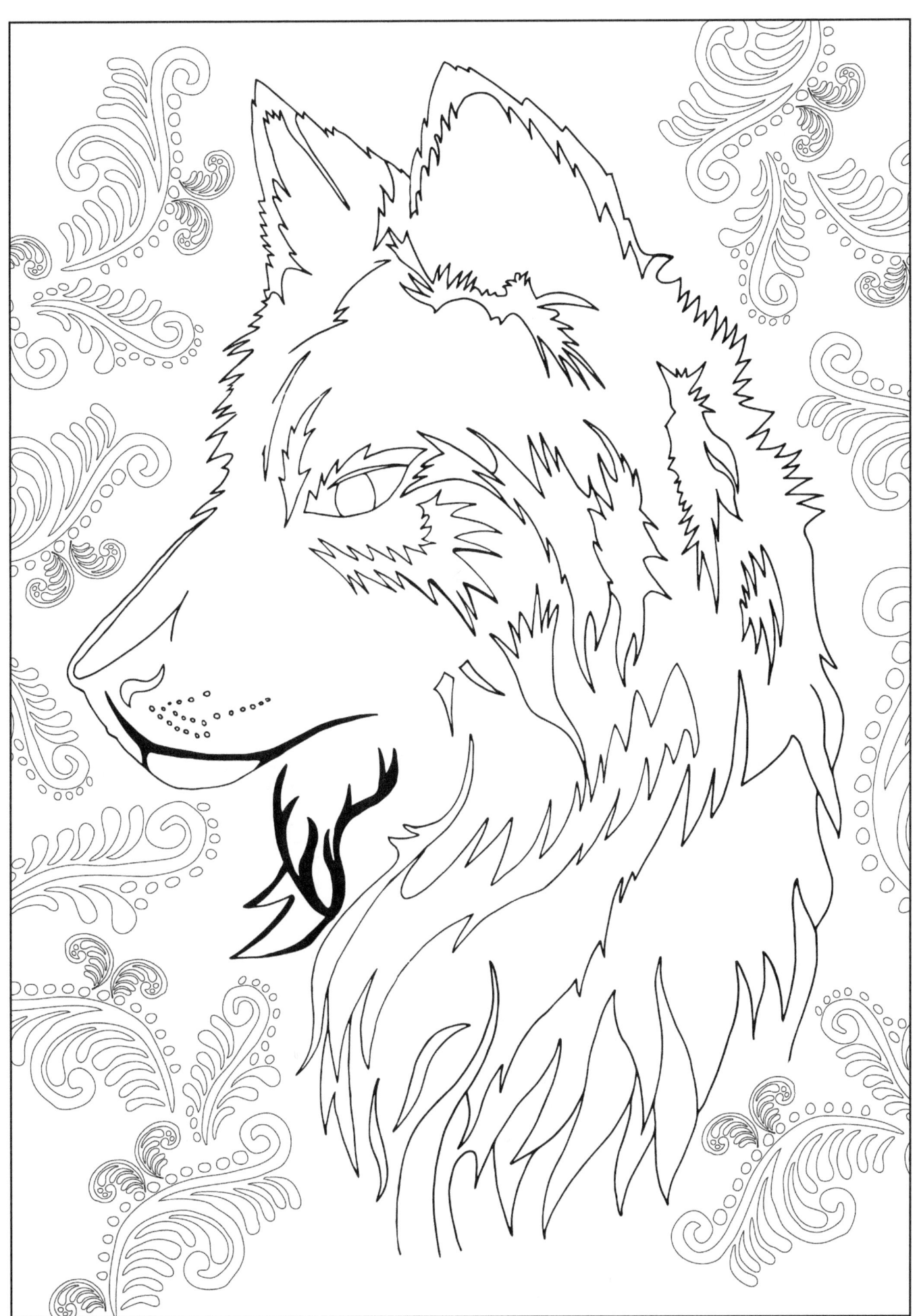

© 2021 Demitrius Lam. All rights reserved.

© 2021 Demitrius Lam. All rights reserved.

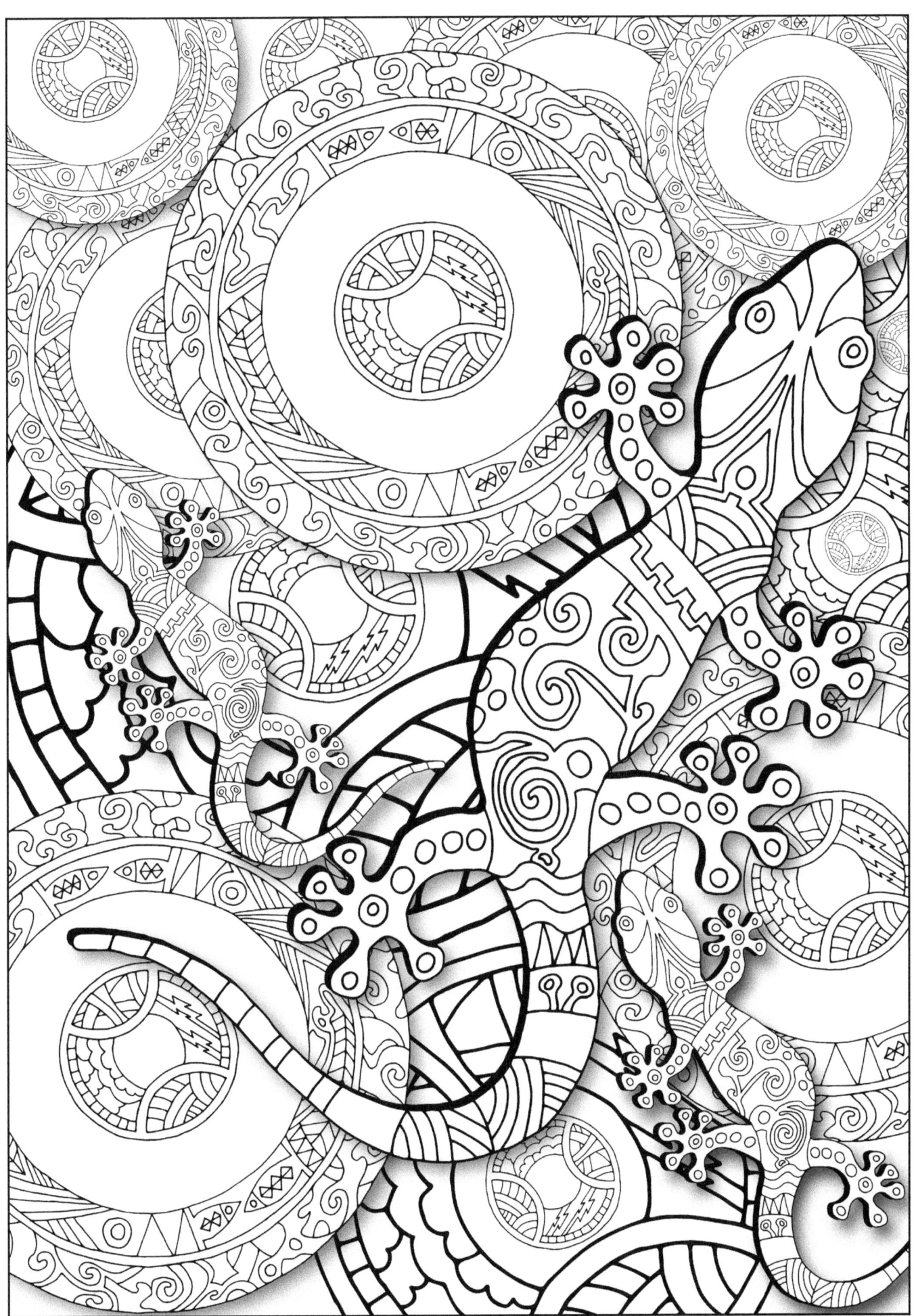
© 2021 Demitrius Lam. All rights reserved.

© 2021 Demitrius Lam. All rights reserved.

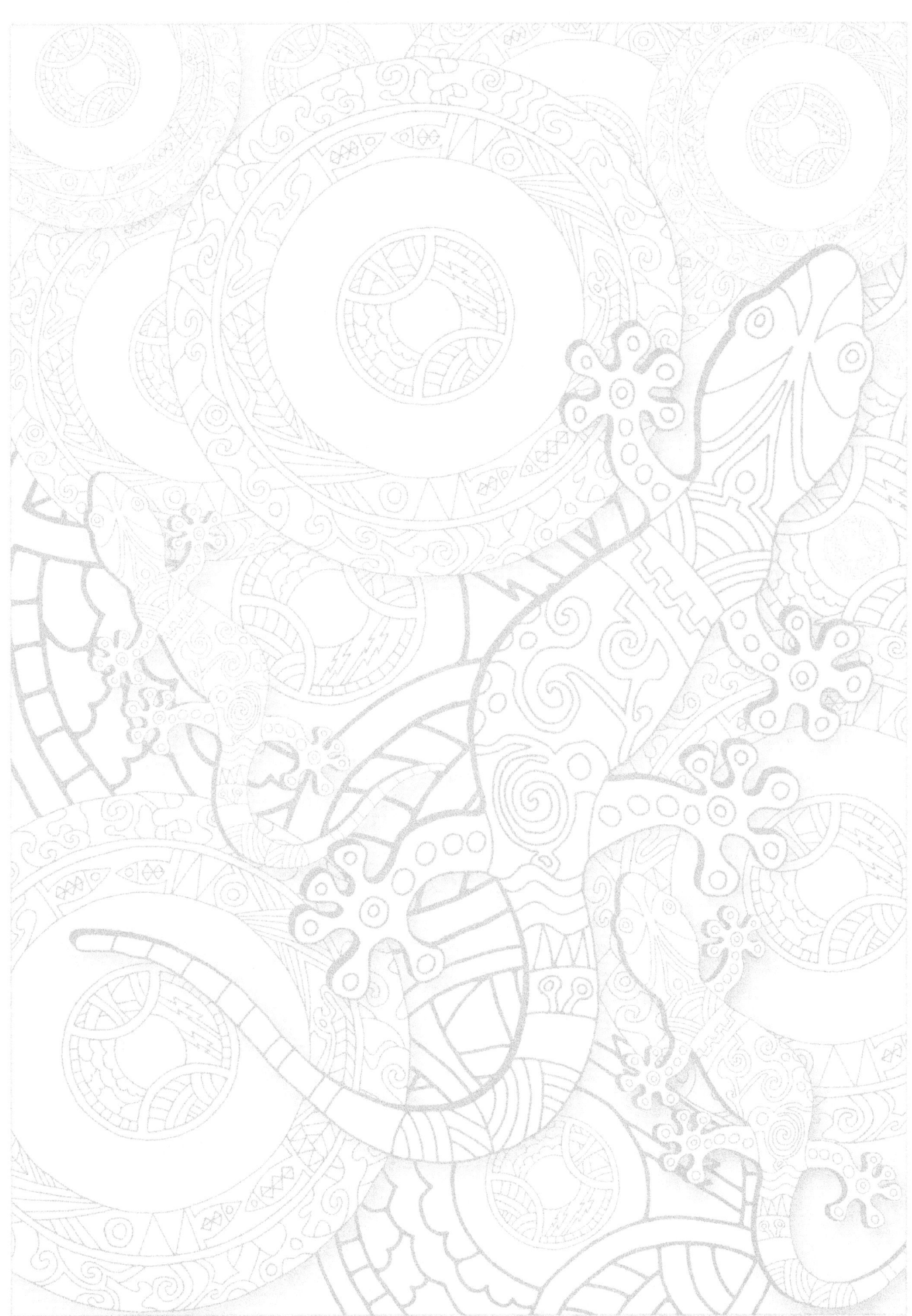

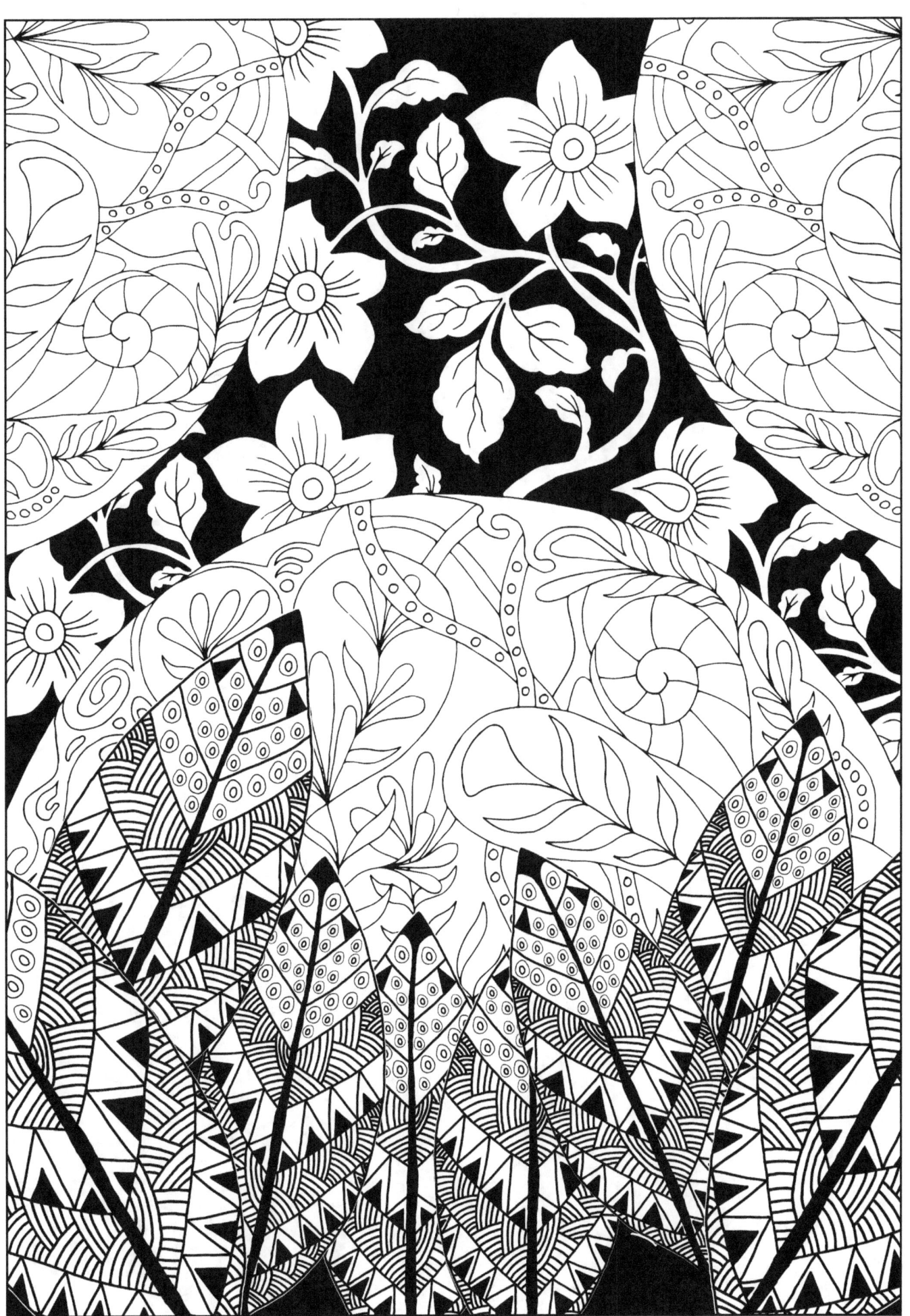

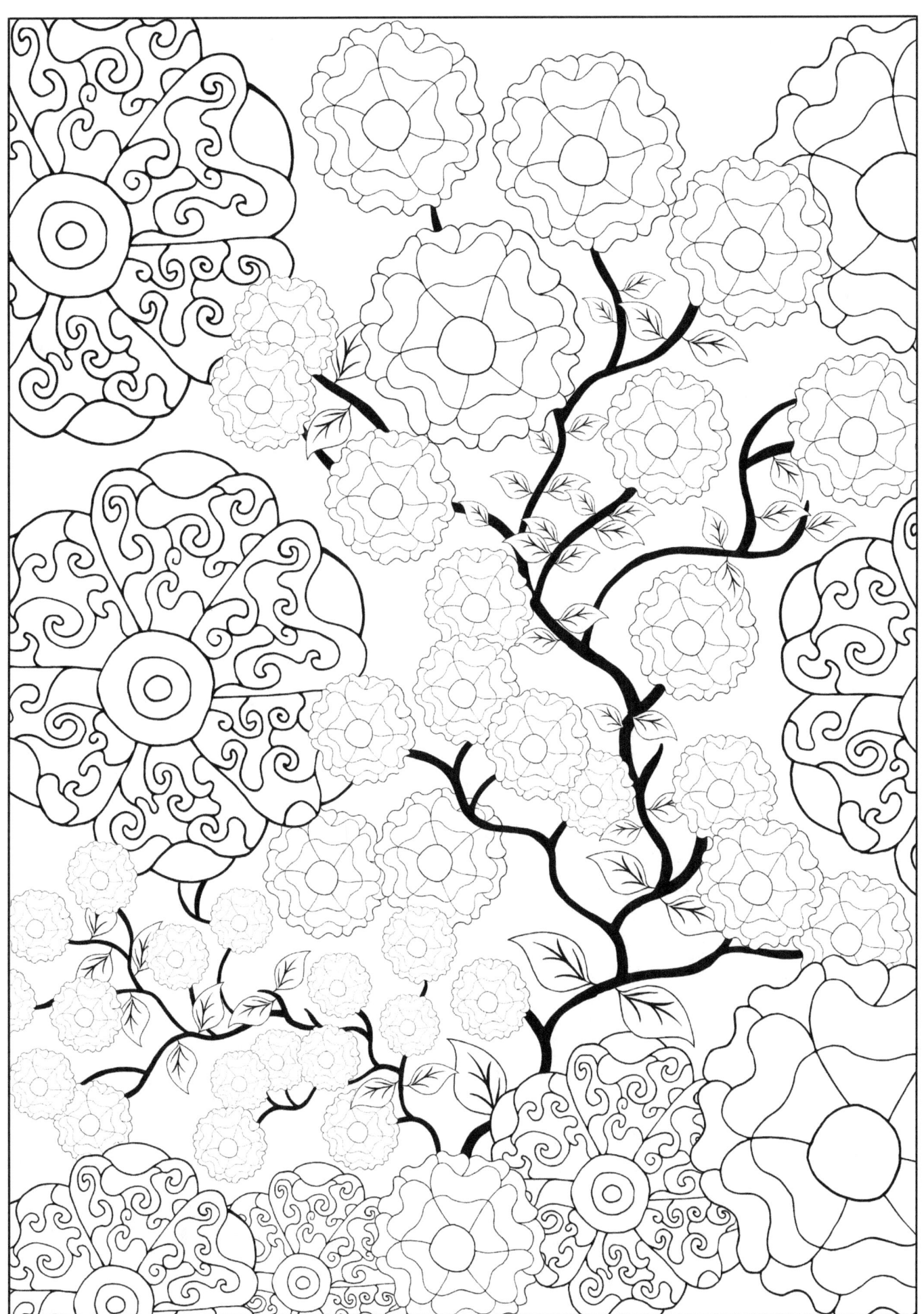

© 2021 Demitrius Lam. All rights reserved.

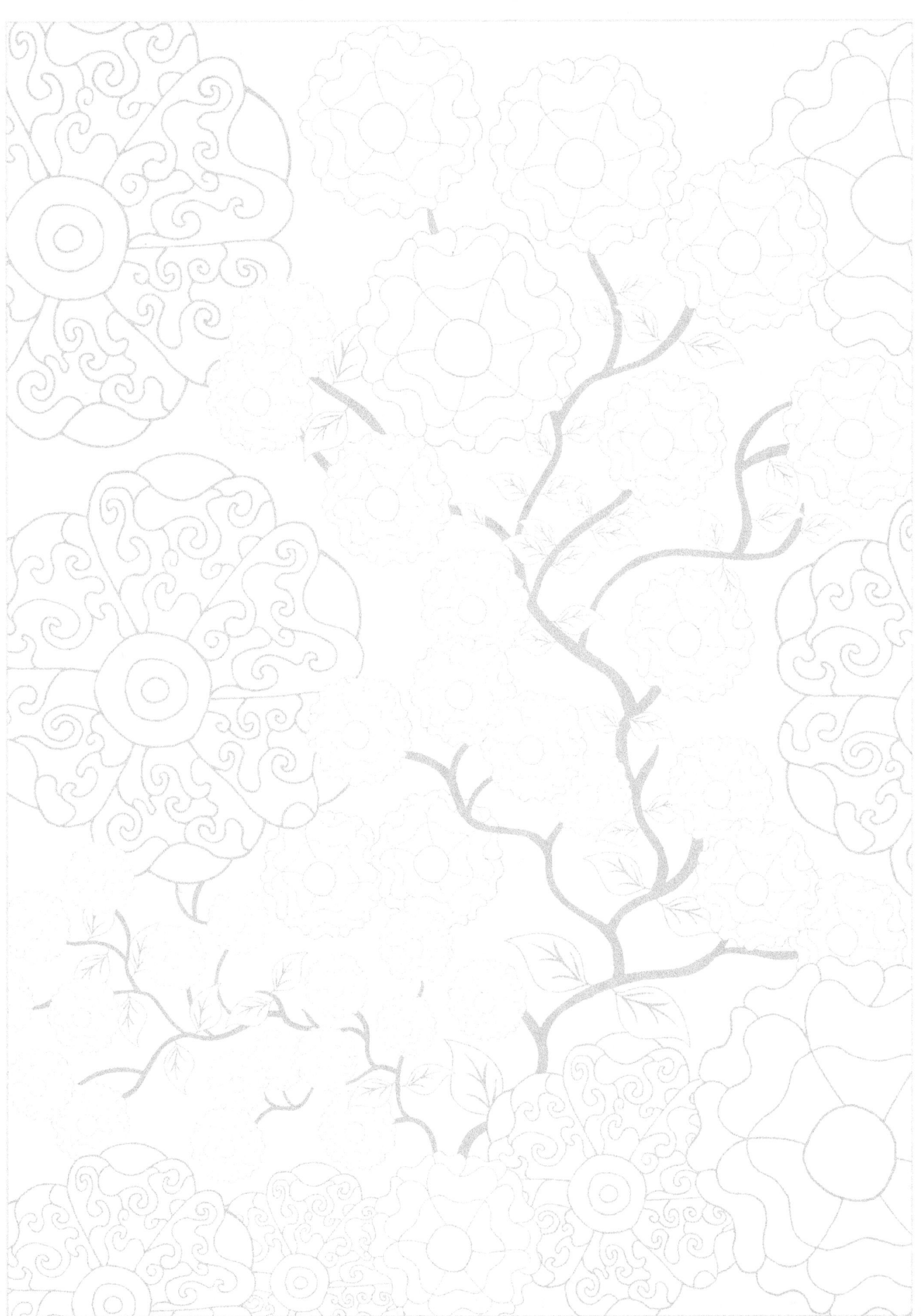

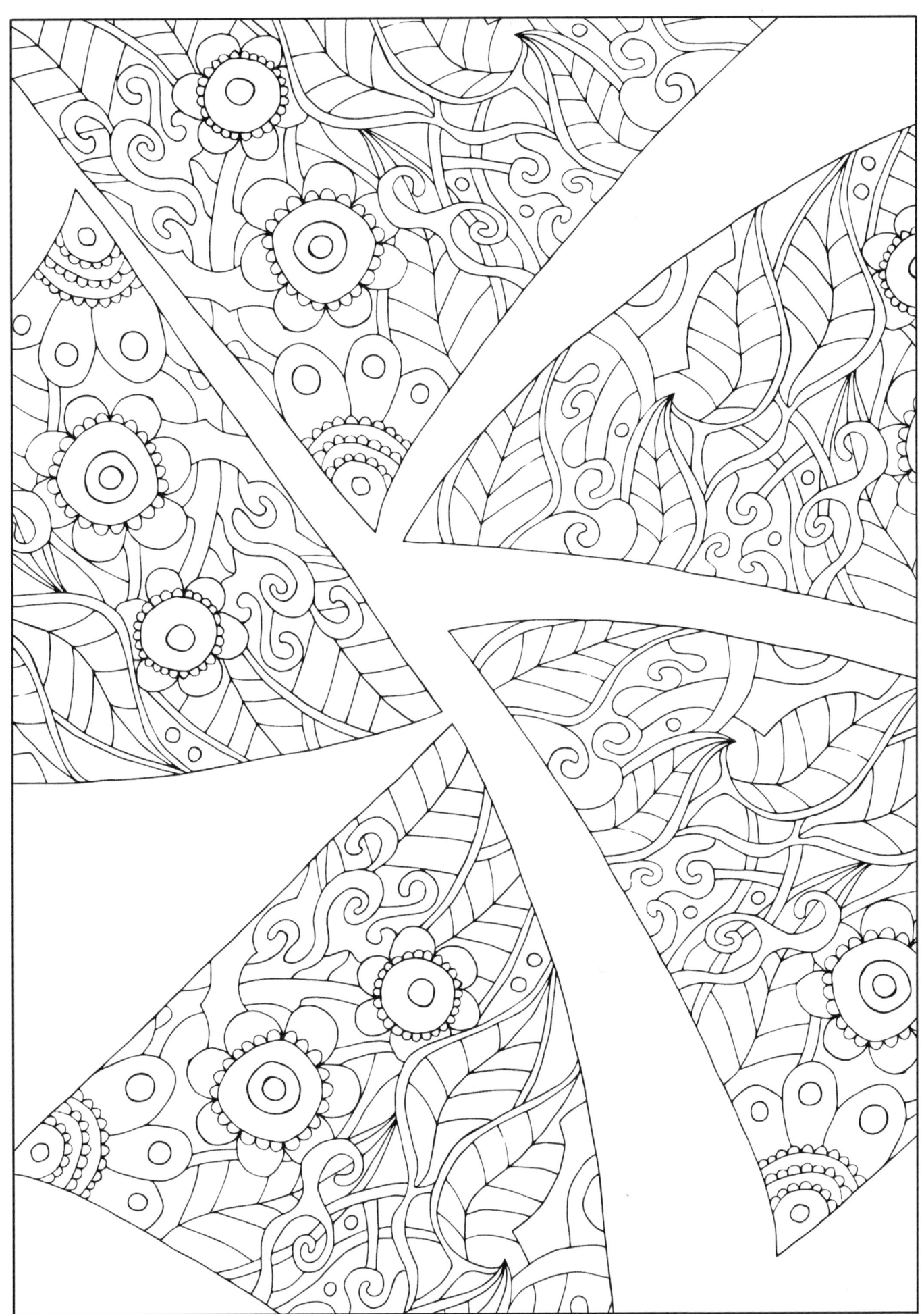
© 2021 Demitrius Lam. All rights reserved.

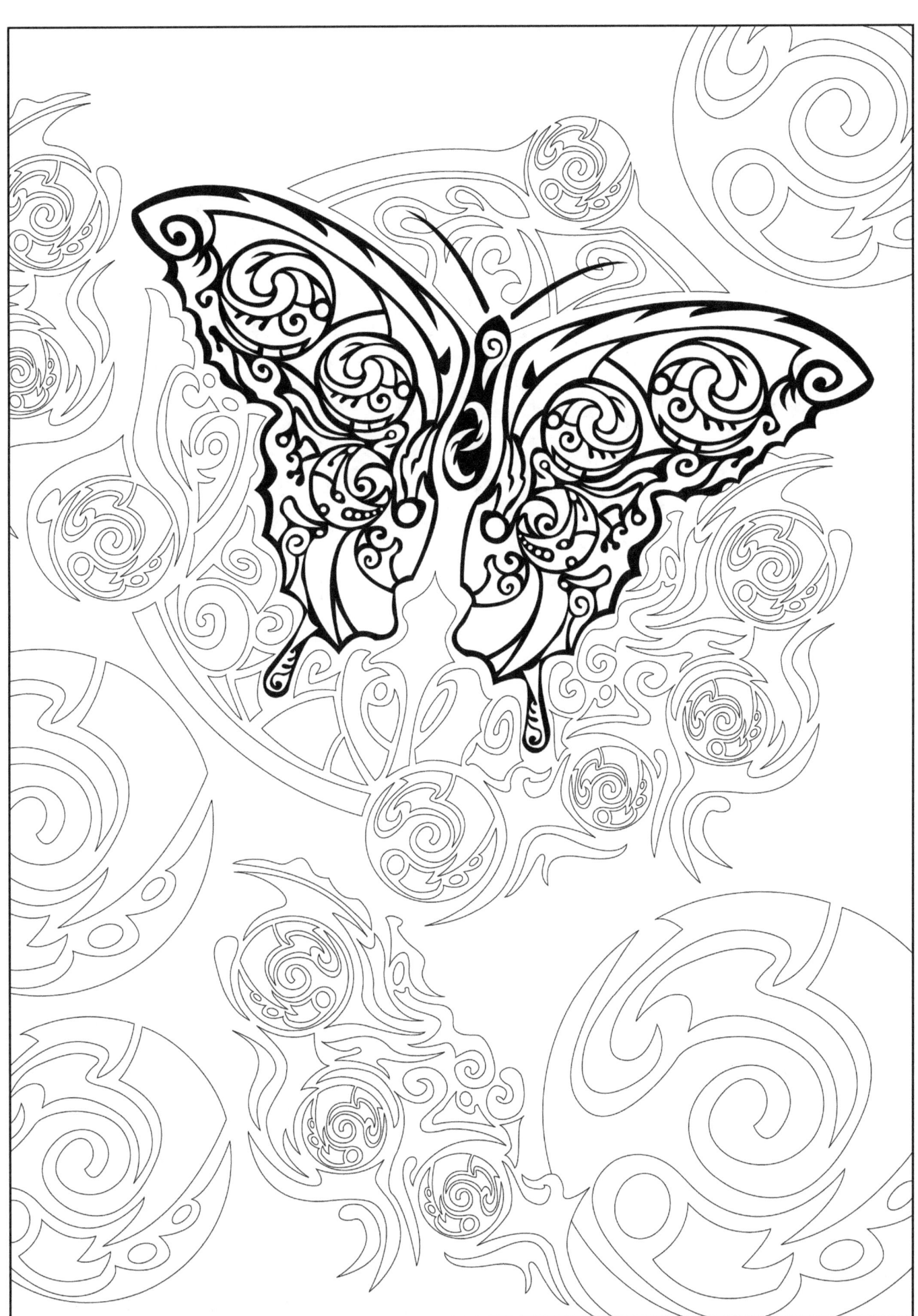

© 2021 Demitrius Lam. All rights reserved.

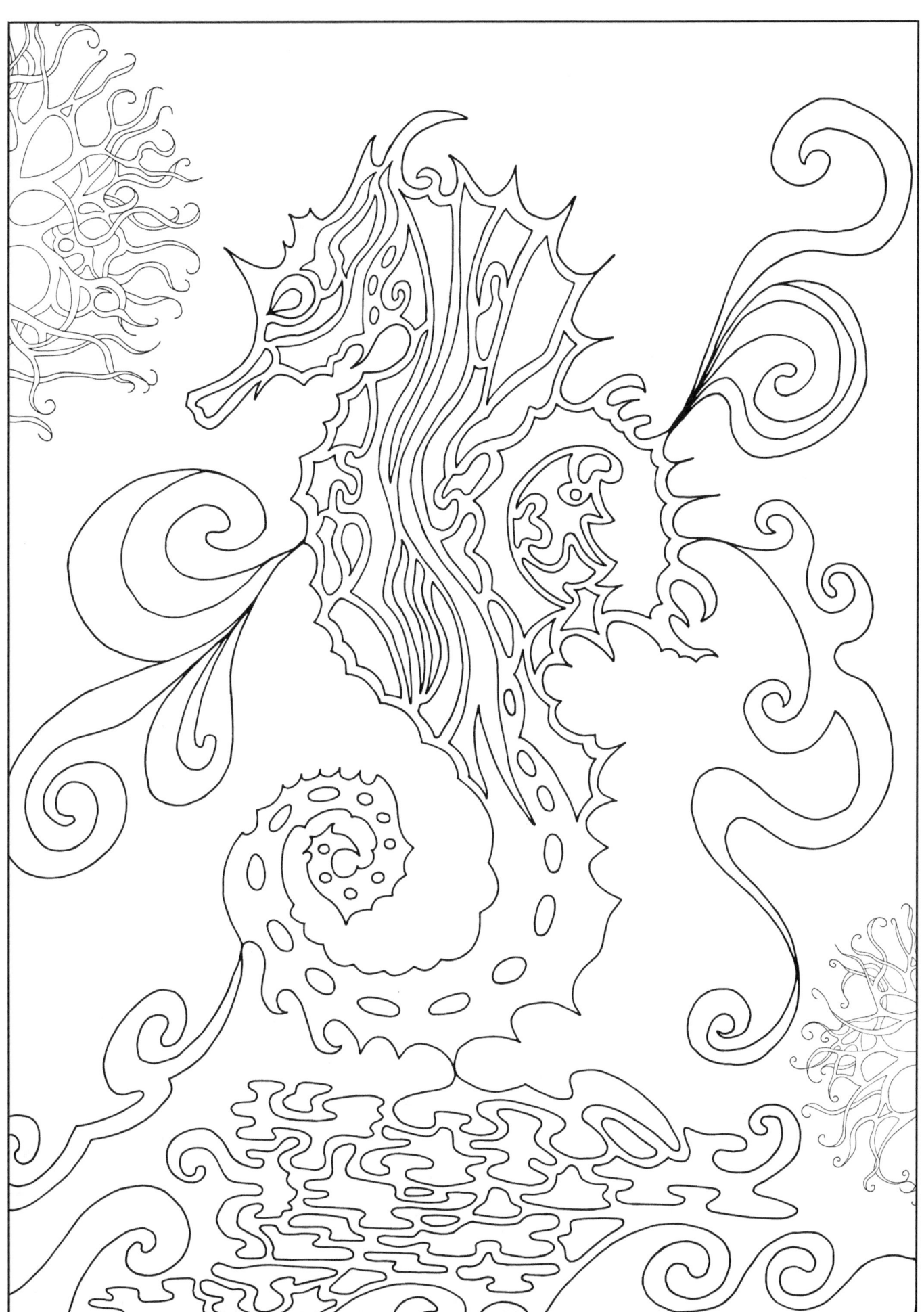

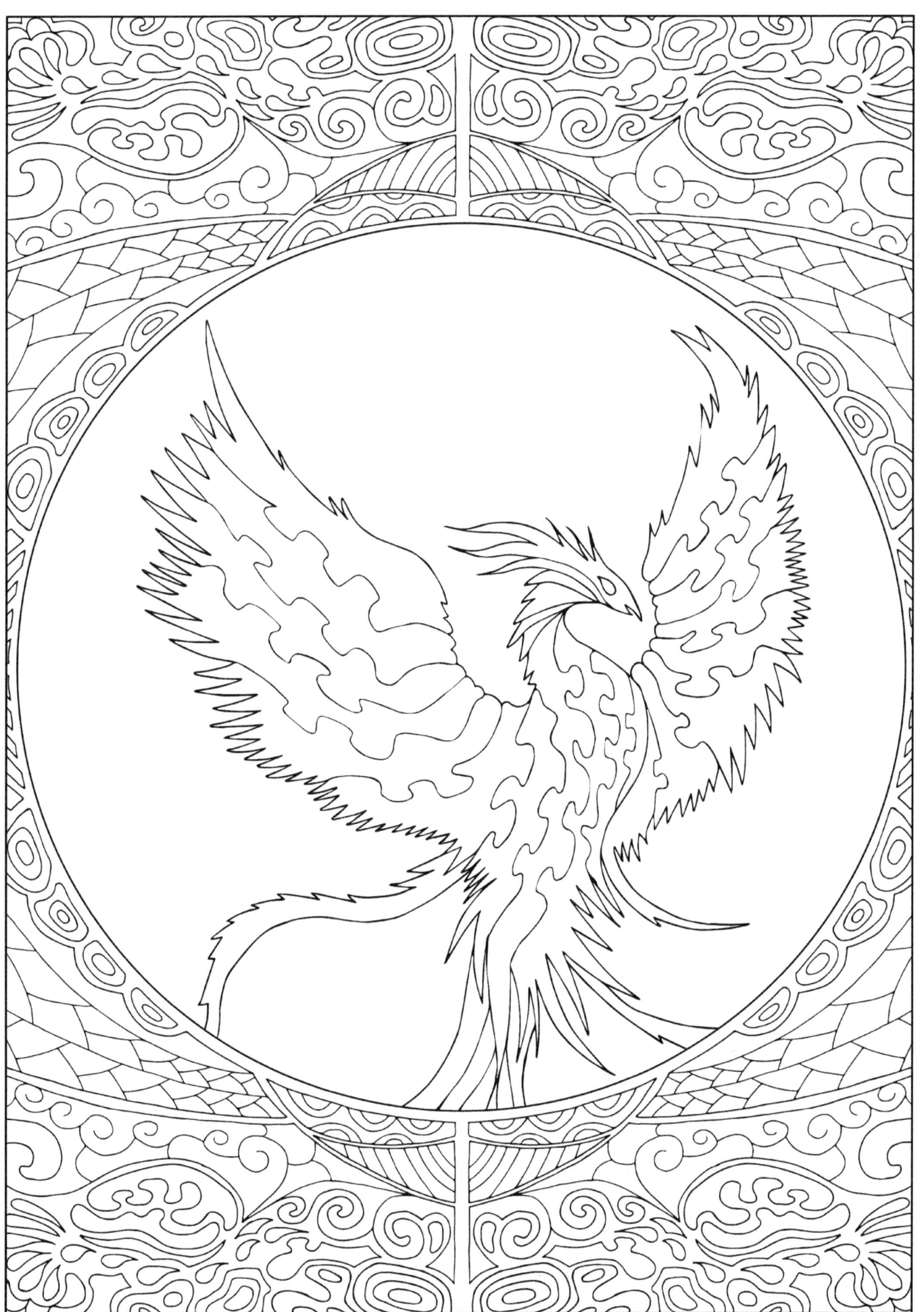
© 2021 Demitrius Lam. All rights reserved.

© 2021 Demitrius Lam. All rights reserved.

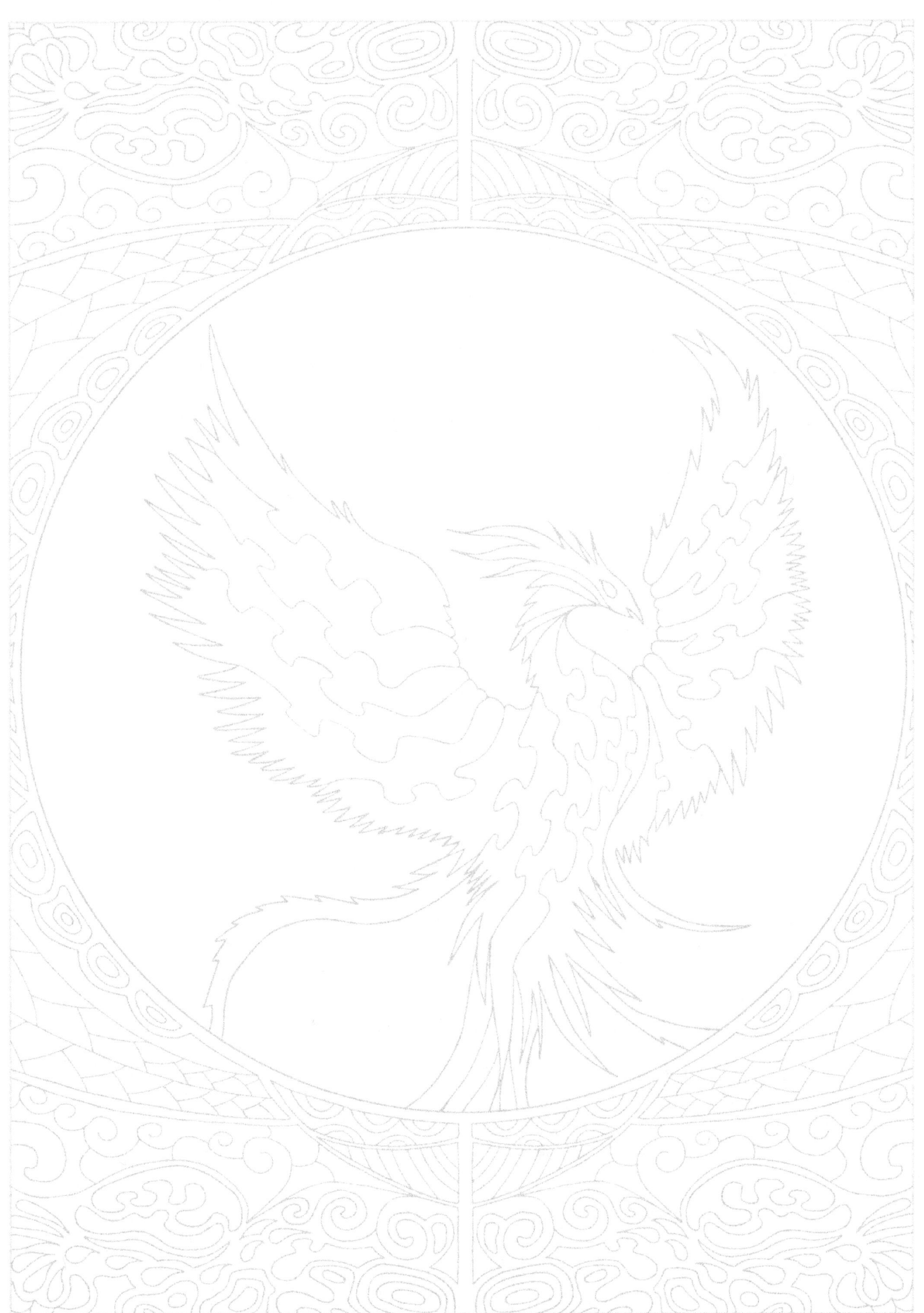

© 2021 Demitrius Lam. All rights reserved.

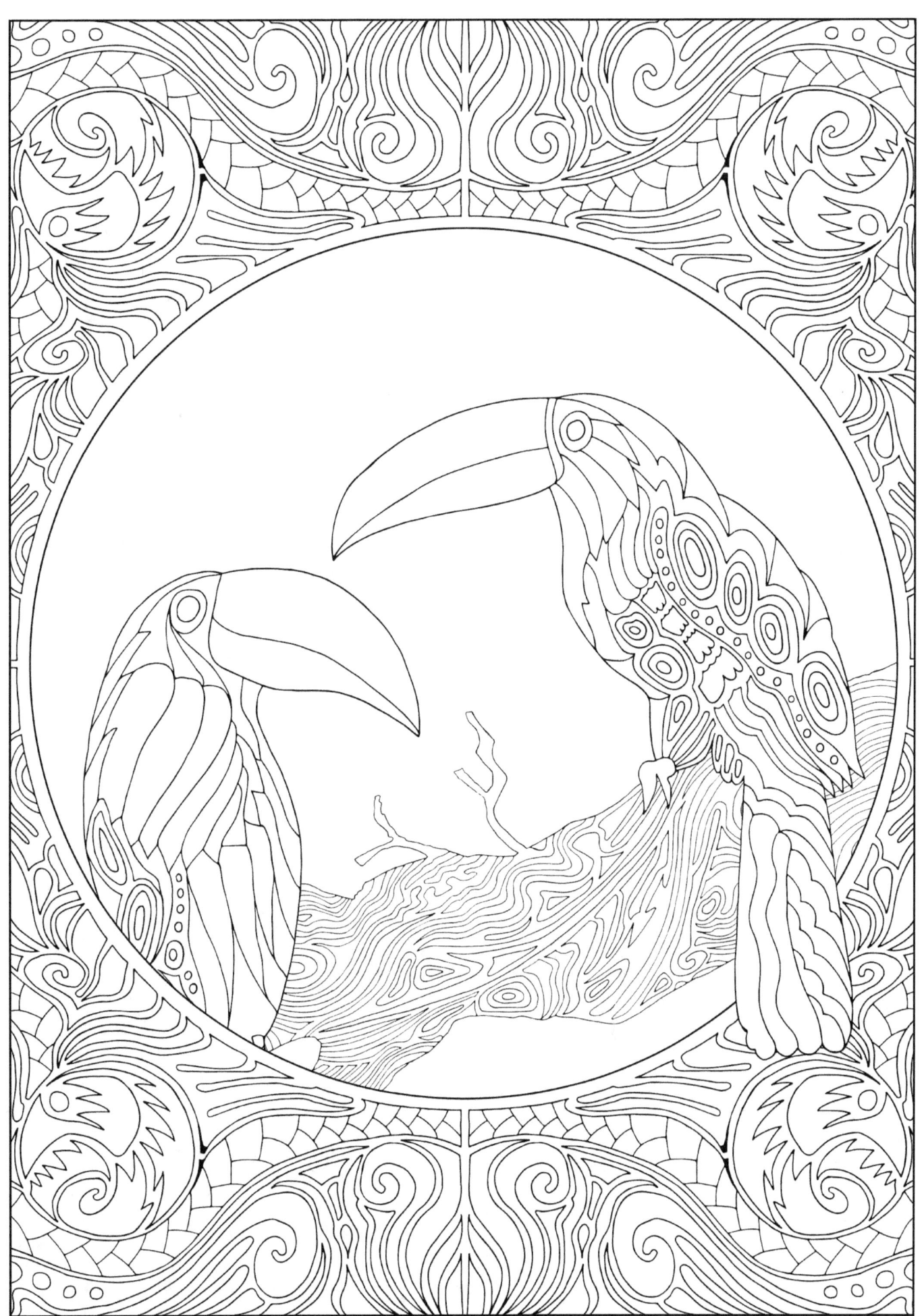

© 2021 Demitrius Lam. All rights reserved.

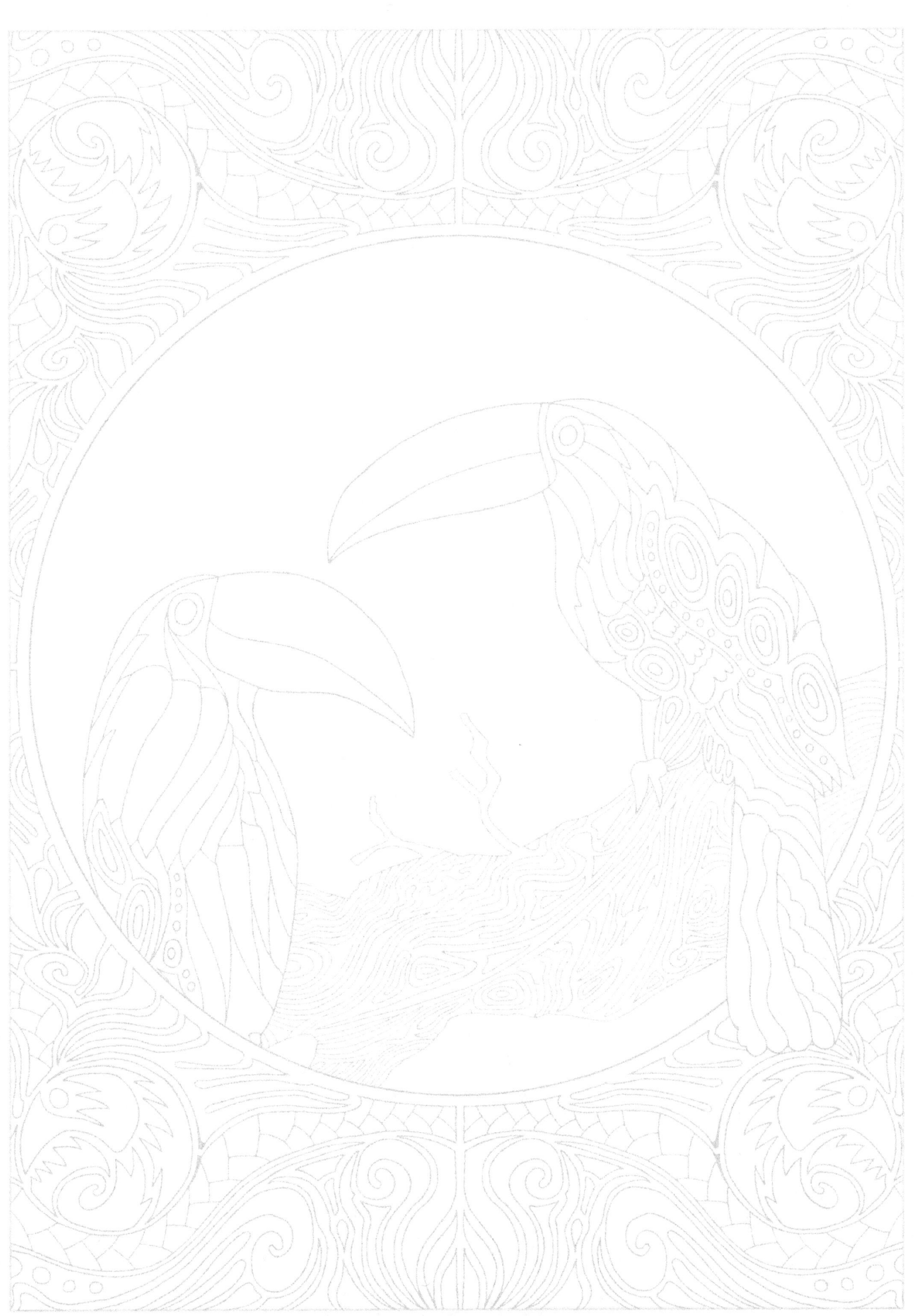

© 2021 Demitrius Lam. All rights reserved.

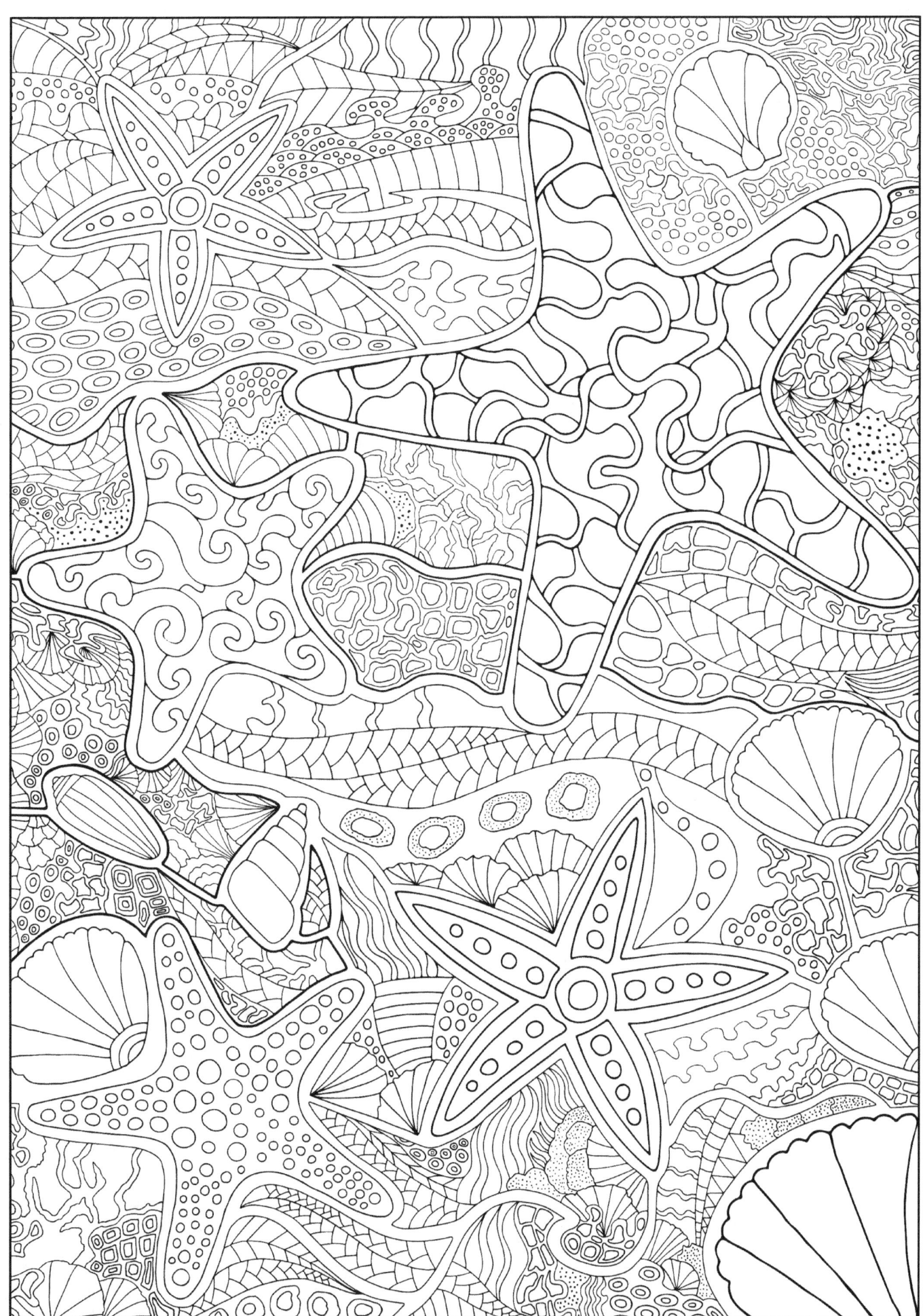

© 2021 Demitrius Lam. All rights reserved.

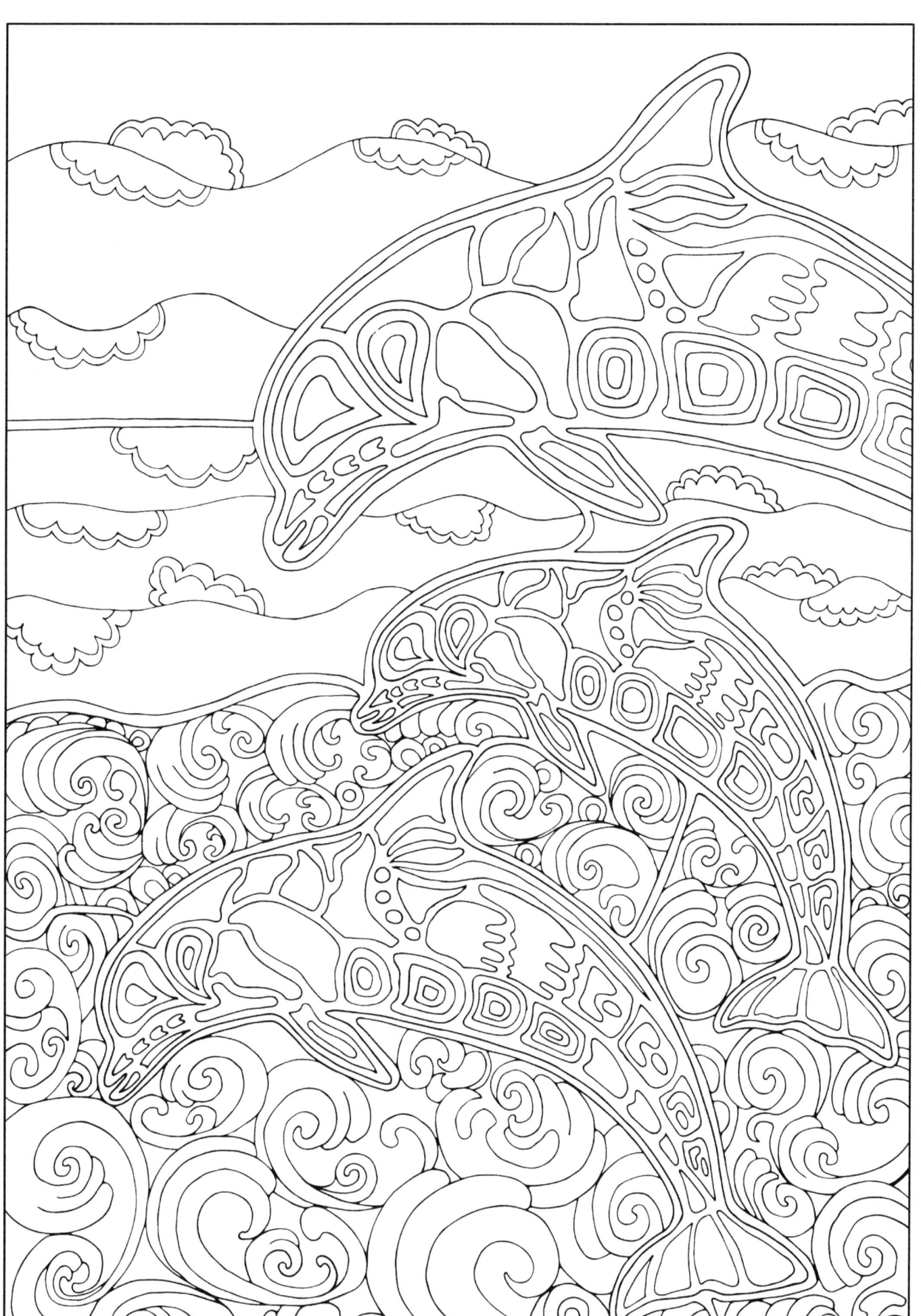

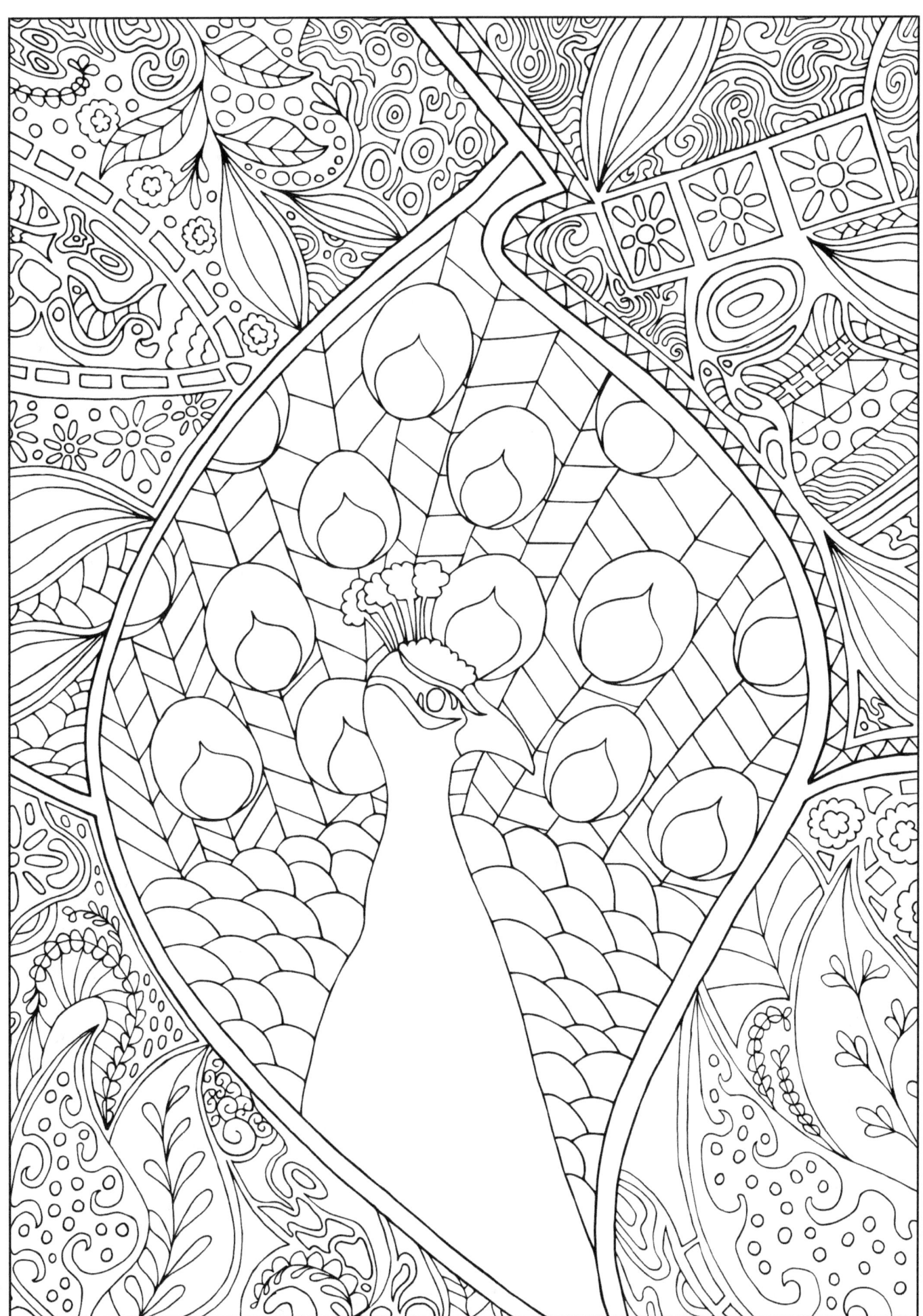
© 2021 Demitrius Lam. All rights reserved.

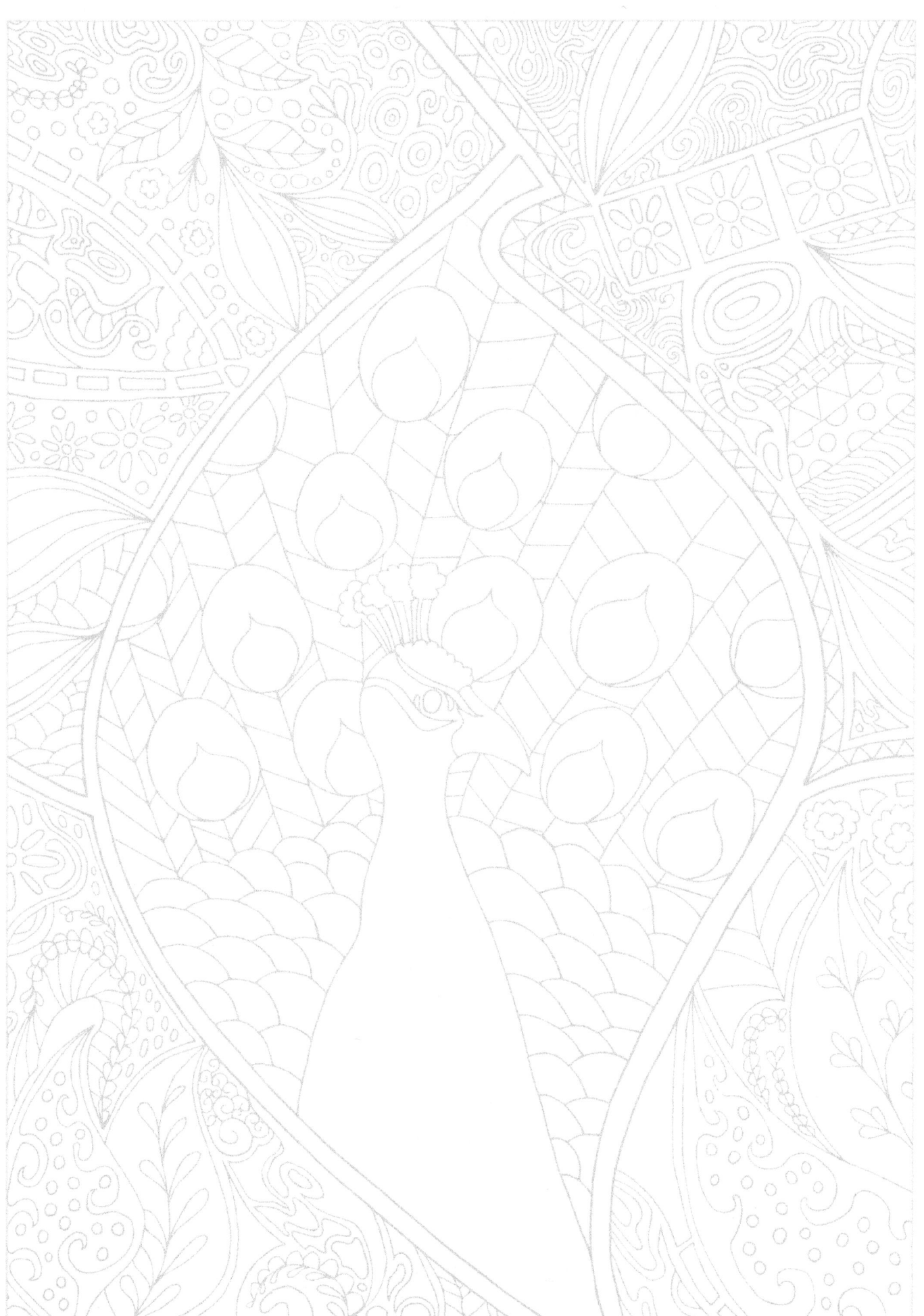

© 2021 Demitrius Lam. All rights reserved.

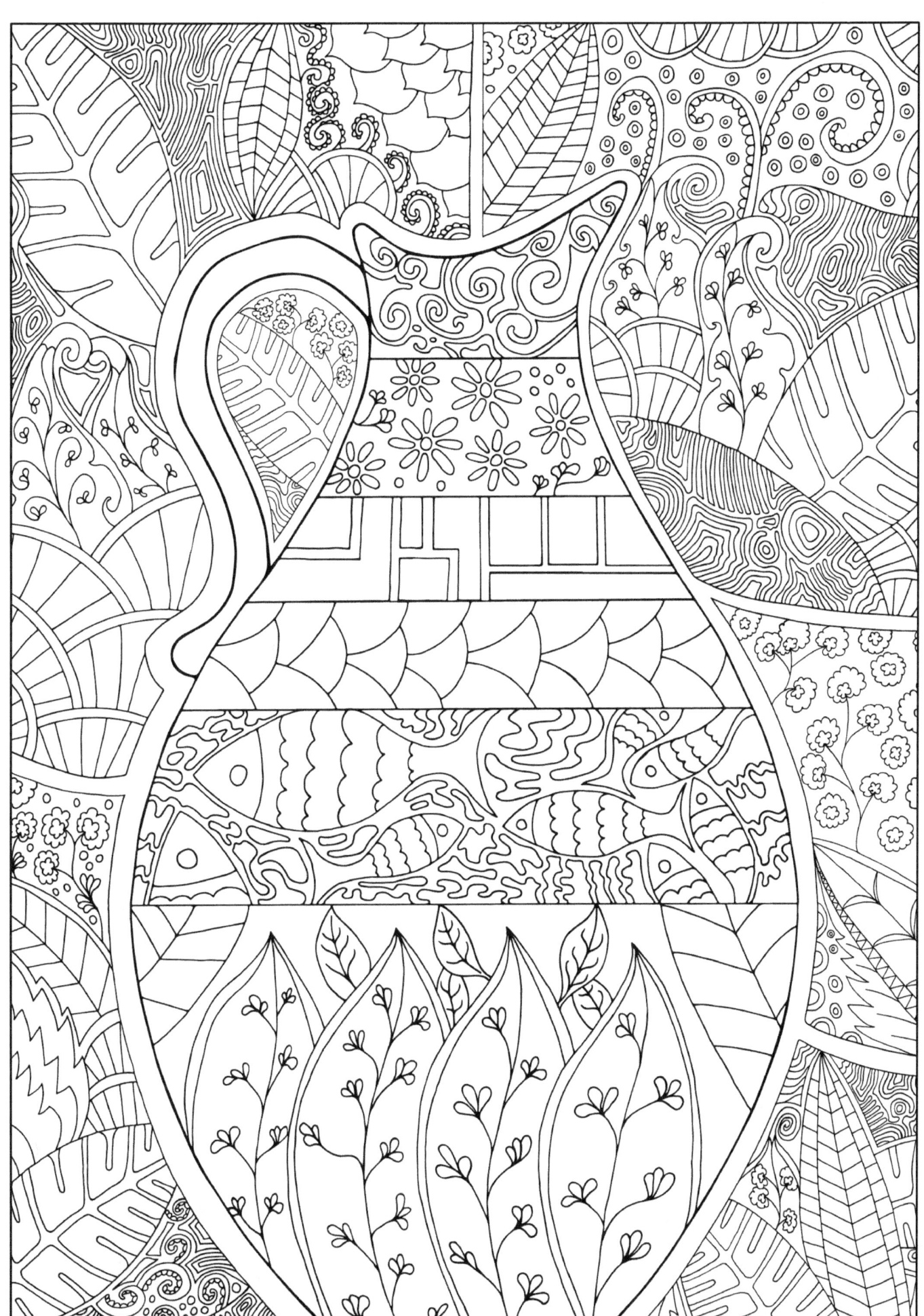

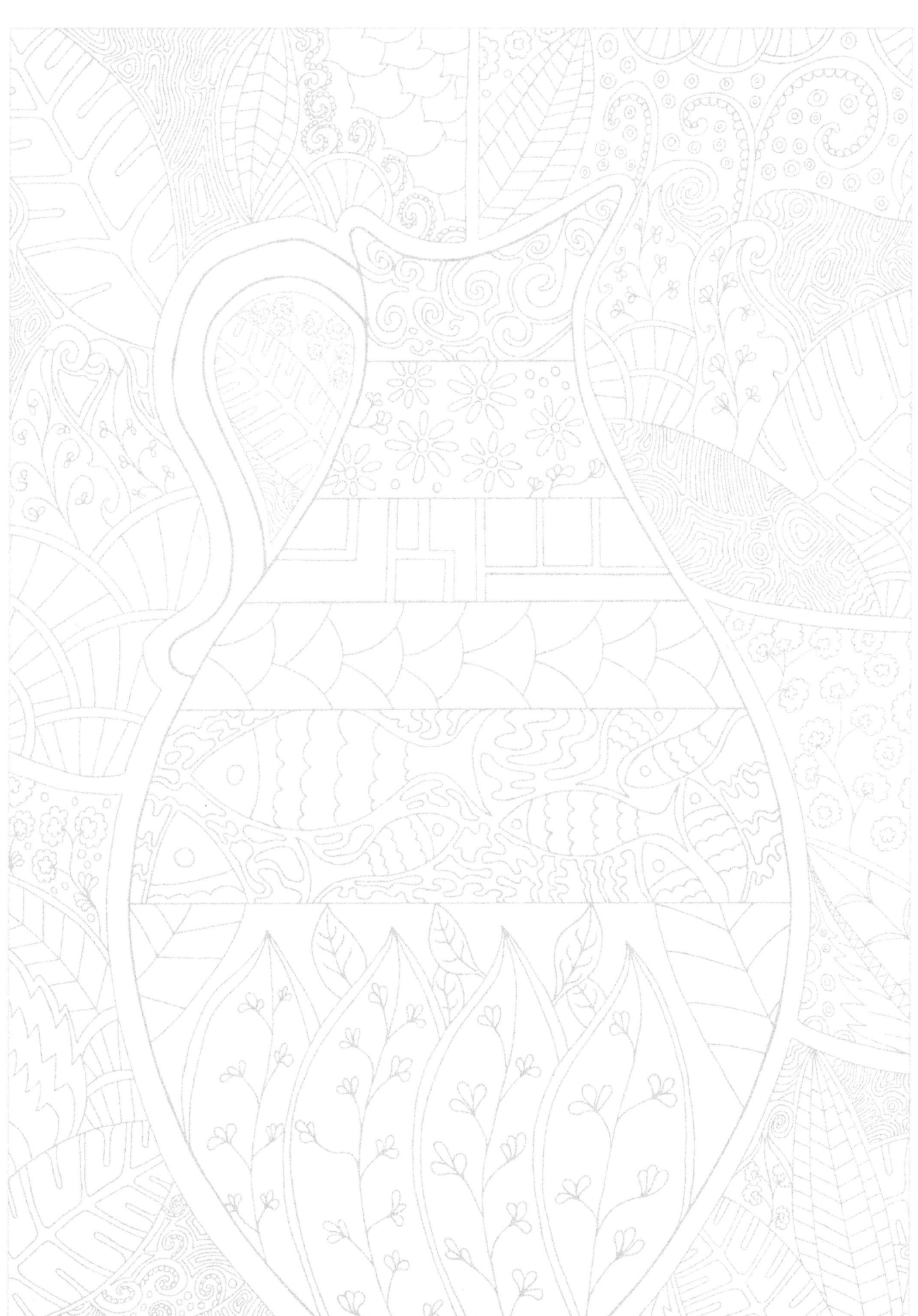

© 2021 Demitrius Lam. All rights reserved.

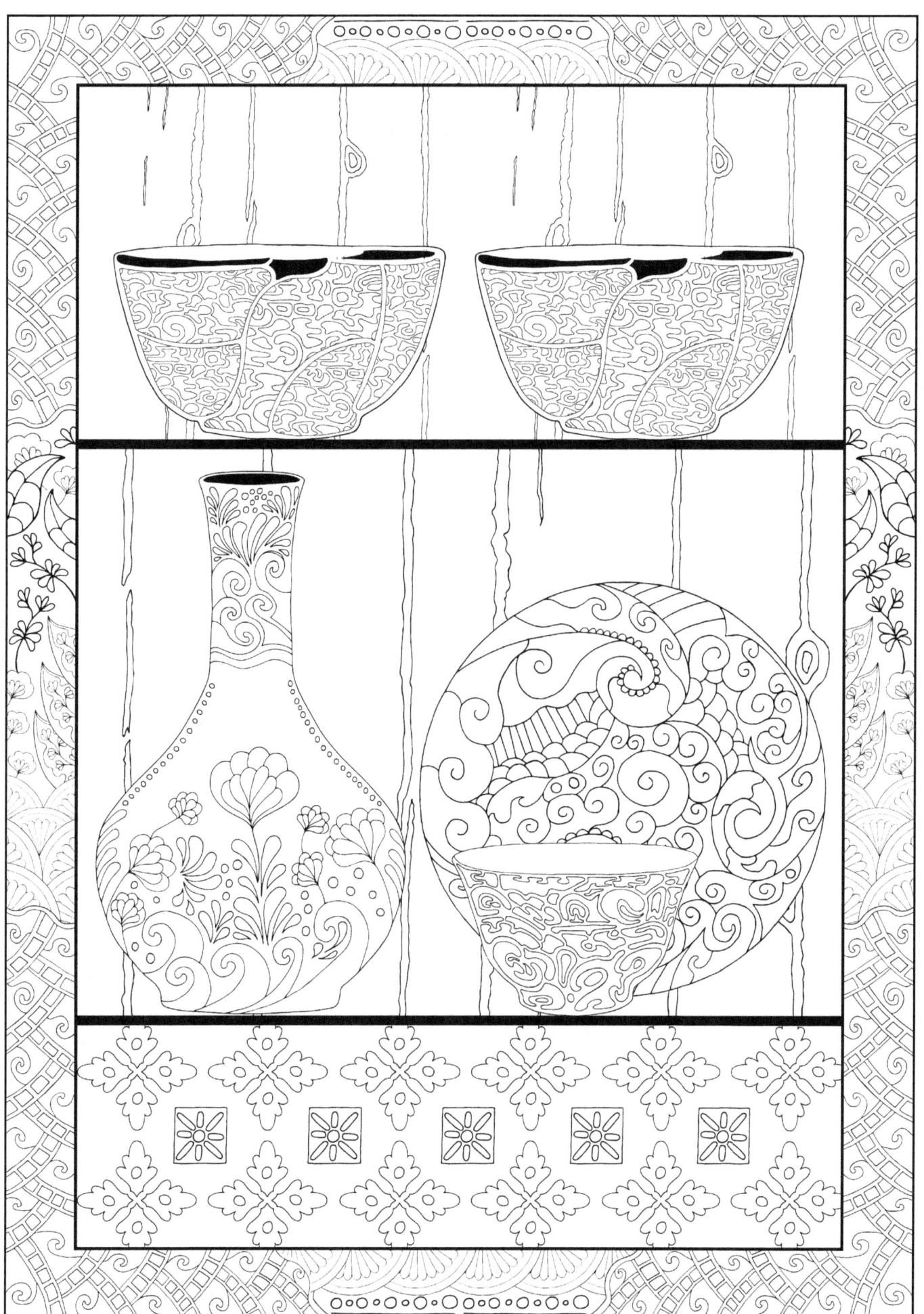

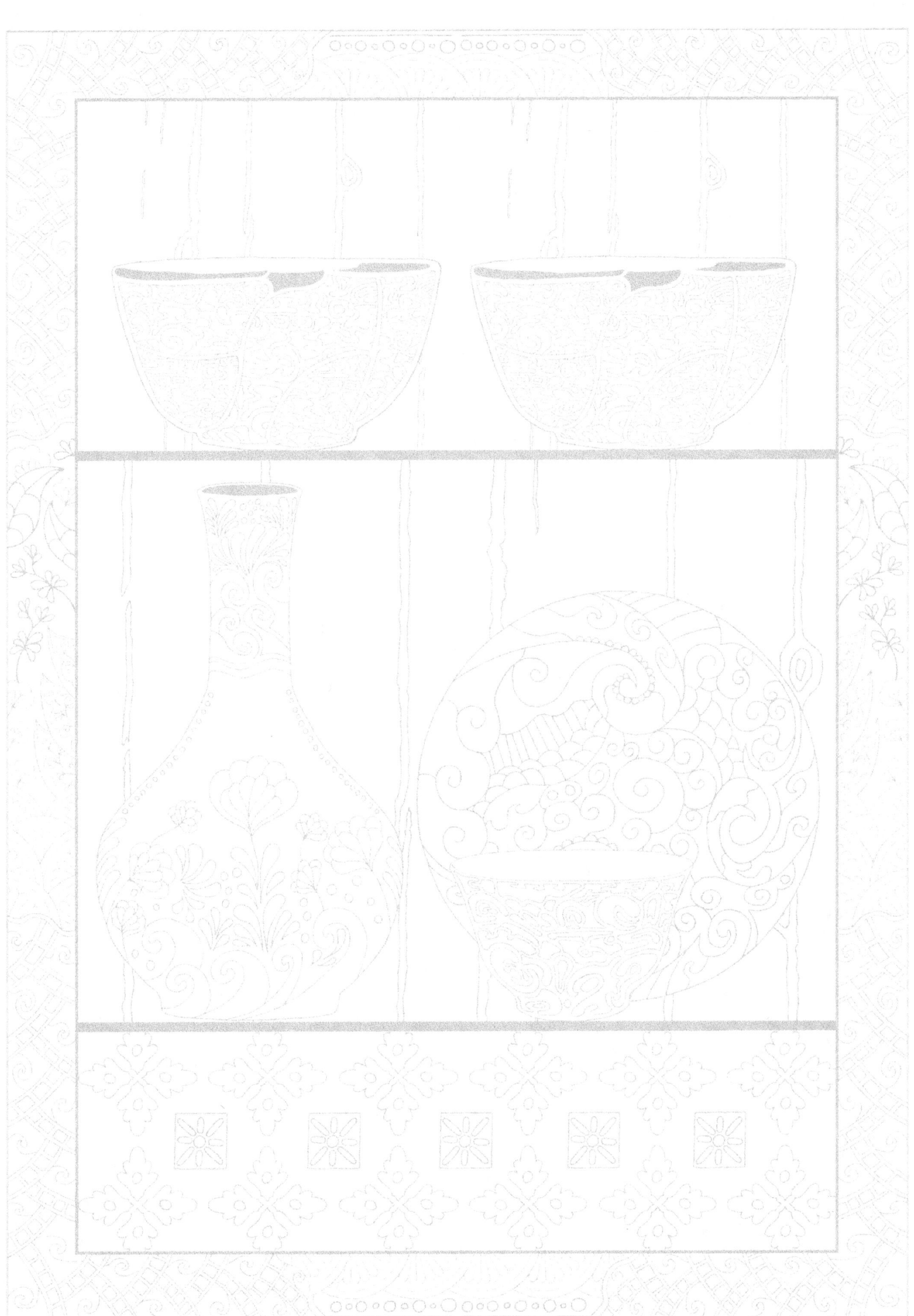

© 2021 Demitrius Lam. All rights reserved.

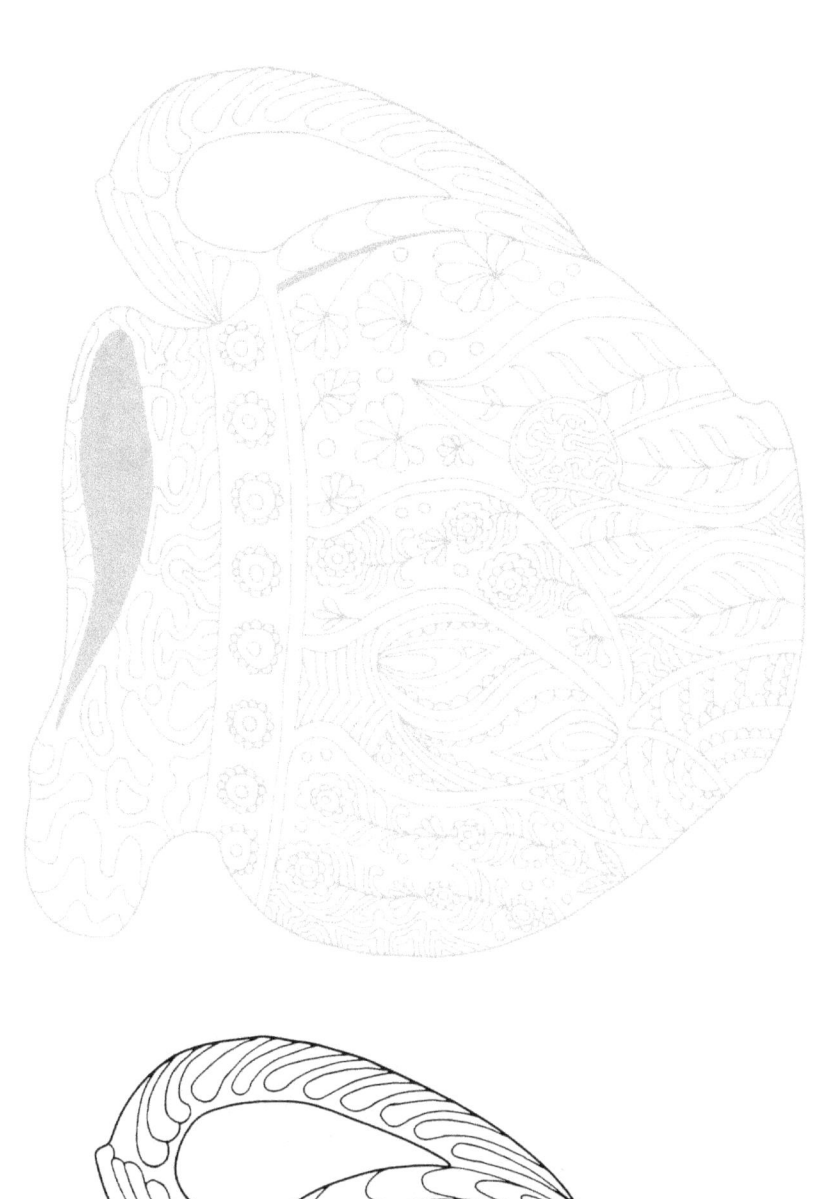
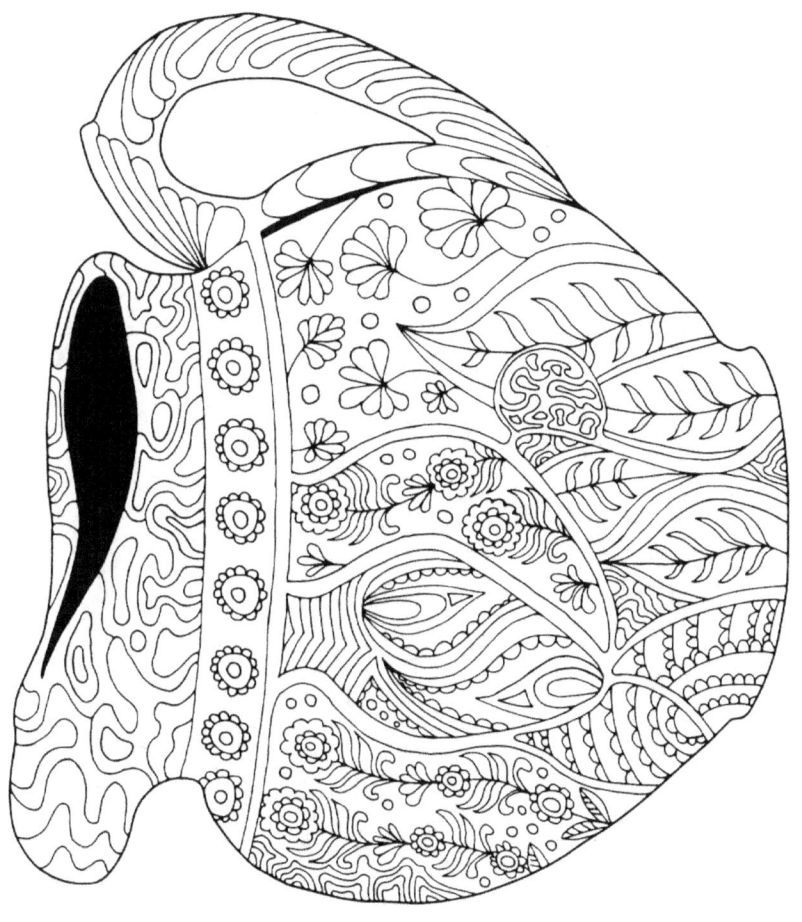

www.ingramcontent.com/pod-product-compliance
Lightning Source LLC
Chambersburg PA
CBHW062359220526
45472CB00008B/1874